The Longest Interurban Charter

Larry Plachno

The Longest Interurban Charter

by Larry Plachno

Copyright © 1988 by Transportation Trails

All Rights Reserved

No part of this book may be reproduced in any manner whatsoever without written permission from the publisher, except in the case of brief quotations embodied in reviews and articles.

For information write to:

Transportation Trails
National Bus Trader, Inc.
9698 West Judson Road
Polo, Illinois 61064
(815) 946-2341

First Printing: September, 1988
Manufactured in the United States of America

Library of Congress Cataloging in Publication Data

Plachno, Larry, 1943–
  The longest interurban charter / Larry Plachno,
    p.   cm.
  Bibliography: p.
  Includes index.
  ISBN 0-933449-08-9
  1. United States—Description and travel—1900-1920. 2. Street-railroads—United States—History—20th century. 3. Railroad travel—United States—History—20th century. 4. Utica (N.Y.)—History. I. Title.
  E168.P68 1988
  973.91—dc19   88-24784
                              CIP

Publisher's Credits

electronic typesetting and page layout: National Bus Trader, Inc., Polo, Illinois.
silhouette drawing of car 502: J.R. McFarlane.
route maps: Larry Plachno.
printing and binding: Rochelle Printing Co., Rochelle, Illinois.

Table of Contents

Foreword 5
Acknowledgements 7
Utica in 1910 *(by Douglas M. Preston)* 9
1 **The Interurban Network** 13
2 **Planning and Preparations** 19
  First Itinerary and Final Itinerary 20
  C. Loomis Allen 28
3 **The Electric Interurban Odyssey** 31
  Map showing route of the 1910 tour 30
  Map of Interurbans in the Cleveland area 44
  Map of Interurbans in the Toledo area 64
4 **Records And Accomplishments** 75
  Interurban Lines Covered and Mileage 76
  Final Report of the Treasurer of the Trolley Tour 86
Epilogue 89
Notes 91
Bibliography 93
Index 95

To Jackie

*In appreciation for unending support
and countless hours of proofreading*

Most of the longer trips by interurban were generally made during the summer months. Like most railroads in the Midwest, the interurban lines were subject to delays from snow during the winter months and flooding during the spring. This photo shows a Lake Shore Electric snowplow clearing the way for a passenger car in Sandusky, Ohio following a storm on February 14, 1909. FOLLETT HOUSE MUSEUM.

Foreword

At 10:30 a.m. on Tuesday, May 10, 1910, a group of 21 businessmen from Utica, New York boarded a chartered interurban car and set off on a two week trip that could only be classed as an adventure.

Their reasons for making this trip were primarily civic and business. They intended to make a personal inspection of several major Midwestern cities to look for innovative civic and public works concepts that could be of value to Utica. They also were interested in finding ideas that could be used back home for encouraging both businesses and conventions to select Utica as a location.

What made the purpose of this trip particularly unique was that the group did not promote Utica outright and try to sell its benefits. Instead, they looked for ideas where they went. They were anxious to learn about other communities and how their accomplishments might be applied to their home city. In most places the Utica group complimented the local community for its achievements. This attitude made a very favorable impression on civic groups met along the way. In addition, it set the all-time record for distance covered by an interurban charter. It was also instrumental in closing a track gap in the interurban network. No later group or charter car was ever able to duplicate this distance. Their record still stands today.

What made this trip specially interesting is that it operated over approximately 28 different interurban lines in six different states. In spite of the variety of lines and distance covered, the group was able to maintain a very rigid schedule that provided for travel, meals, sightseeing, side trips and sleep at hotels along the way. Moreover, the chartered car was able to operate on its own without assistance on all but one line. Yet, it operated entirely on electric lines and under electric power on the entire trip.

What made this trip particularly historic is that the journey took place at a time that must be called the peak of the interurban era. The preceding decade had witnessed a major building boom in electric interurban railways. This construction of new lines had only recently created the Midwest network of interurban track that would be used by the Utica group. Optimism was high and the interurbans were enjoying a popularity and acceptance that would not long remain.

The Utica group visited virtually every major city in the six-state area that was an important junction point in the interurban network. Included were Indianapolis, Dayton, Columbus, Fort Wayne, Lima, Toledo, Detroit, Cleveland, Buffalo, Rochester and Syracuse. The interurban lines traversed represented a wide variety from small to large and from prosperous to bankrupt. Among the more popular lines were the Buffalo & Lake Erie Traction; Cleveland, Painesville & Eastern; Cleveland, Southwestern & Columbus; Columbus, Delaware & Marion; Ohio Electric Railway; Terre Haute, Indianapolis & Eastern; Indiana Union Traction; Detroit United; and Lake Shore Electric.

This book is an attempt to document and recreate the adventure of the Utica Electric Railway Tour of 1910 and to look at the interconnected interurban network when it was young, dynamic and optimistic.

Larry Plachno
Polo, Illinois
April 28, 1988

Ohio Electric Railway car 81 poses in Lima, Ohio on Grand Avenue in front of the Lima Barn. This car was originally built in 1906 by the Cincinnati Car Co. for the Fort Wayne, Van Wert & Lima Traction Company. Through a lease arrangement, both the line and the car were taken over by the Ohio Electric in 1907. BRADLEY-HARNISH COLLECTION FROM THE LATE DR. R.C. PRUGH.

Rochester, Syracuse & Eastern car 114 is shown on Water Street at the Congress Hall Hotel in Lyons, New York. This was the first interurban car into Lyons from the west. The photo was taken on August 18, 1906. SHELDEN S. KING COLLECTION.

6 • *The Longest Interurban Charter*

Acknowledgements

From a historical perspective, the big question regarding the 1910 adventure of the Utica businessmen is not whether the trip was generally known, but rather why it has never been fully explained and documented.

The fact that the trip took place has never been subject to question. At least two contemporary trade magazines reported on the trip and there were numerous newspaper articles in 1910, particularly in Utica. In more recent years, the trip has been mentioned in at least eight books and two periodicals.[1] With the exception of one magazine article, all recent mentions of the tour are rather short. It is also interesting that the tour does not appear in any histories of individual interurban lines outside of New York state.

As with most historical books, the author was substantially assisted by numerous individuals who researched, obtained or provided necessary material. A large number of different individuals or historical societies were involved with this effort. The following deserve a special acknowledgement and note of appreciation:

Douglas Preston of the Oneida County Historical Society in Utica provided invaluable assistance. He offered a scrapbook from the 1910 trip that contained a substantial number of news articles written by a member of the group and items obtained during and after the trip. Without this material this book would not have been possible.

J.R. McFarlane of Cape Elizabeth, Maine, author of CERA's Bulletin 44, *The Interurban Lines of Central and Western New York State,* and co-author of *The Rochester, Syracuse & Eastern,* provided invaluable assistance and information. Jim had access to the scrapbook of his friend John Maher, who actually rode on the trip, and offered his unpublished manuscript on the Utica Electric Railway Tour as well as additional research and documentation. He was also responsible for much of the research on C. Loomis Allen. His material covered many of the areas left unanswered by the big scrapbook in Utica and added a great deal to this book.

David Schafer of Lakewood, Ohio, provided invaluable assistance with the official Utica photo of the group and several research documents. He also provided other encouragement and research assistance including substantial background information on C. Loomis Allen.

Shelden S. King of Lyons, New York, author of *The New York State Railways,* provided background information and assisted in locating additional information and photographs.

John C. Claridge of the Erie County Historical Society in Erie provided local news clippings of the trip. He also assisted in researching the events in Erie and Farnham.

Jack Marsh, the executive editor of the *Utica Observer-Dispatch,* graciously granted permission to reprint material and photographs from the newspaper. Dave Dudajek of the *Utica Observer-Dispatch* was responsible for a newspaper article on February 3, 1988, calling attention to this forthcoming book and seeking any additional information and photos.

Stephen Evans of the Montgomery County Historical Society in Dayton provided local news clippings on the trip. He also assisted in trying to track down various events in the Dayton area.

Clarice E. Burd of the Greater Toledo Office of Tourism & Conventions, Inc. uncovered local news clippings in Toledo. These were particularly valuable since they contain a full listing of passengers and their occupations.

Susan Chiappone of the Silver Creek, New York office of the *Dunkirk Evening Observer* published a notice in the newspaper seeking additional information on the delay in Farnham, New York.

Thanks to the following individuals and organizations who provided various clippings and information: Janet Senne of the Erie County Historical Society, Sandusky, Ohio; Barbara Clemsenson of the Western Reserve Historical Society, Cleveland, Ohio; Naomi H. Ryan of the Bucyrus Historical Society, Bucyrus, Ohio; William Reed Gordon, Rochester, New York; Neil Wotherspoon of the Electric Railroader's Association, New York, New York; The Public Library of Columbus & Franklin County, Columbus, Ohio; Eileen J. O'Brien of the New York State Historical Association, Cooperstown, New York; Henry T. Timman, Norwalk, Ohio; Mary F. Bell of the Buffalo and Erie County

Historical Society, Buffalo, New York; Charles R. Evans of the Marion County Historical Society, Marion, Ohio; and Bradner Carlson of The Indianapolis Project, Indianapolis, Indiana.

Thanks to the following individuals and organizations who responded to inquiries and either spent time in research or provided direction for future research: Ben Rohrbeck, West Chester, Pennsylvania; James I. Barstow, Manlius, New York; Rod Varney, San Antonio, Texas; Carol A. Gabriel of the Clark County Historical Society, Springfield, Ohio; Denny Jay of the Center of Science & Industry, Columbus, Ohio; Denyse Clifford and Suzanne Etherington of the Onondaga Historical Association, Syracuse, New York; Alice C. Dalliean of the Detroit Public Library; Walter Font of the Allen County Fort Wayne Historical Society, Fort Wayne, Indiana; Yevetta Y. Beeson of Dayton Newspapers, Inc., Dayton, Ohio; Noraleen Young of the Indiana State Library, Indianapolis, Indiana; Melvin P. Dodge of the Greater Columbus Convention & Visitors Bureau, Columbus, Ohio; Patricia M. Williams of the Greater Syracuse Chamber of Commerce, Syracuse, New York; and Judith A. Ward of the Erie Chamber of Commerce, Erie, Pennsylvania.

Particular thanks goes to those individuals, companies and organizations who opened up their photo collections to us so that we could obtain illustrations to accompany the text of this book. Included are David Schafer, Malcolm D. McCarter, George K. Bradley, Jim McFarlane, Shelden King, David McLellan, Charles Ballard, Jerry Marlette, Helen M. Hansen, Follett House Museum, Rutherford B. Hayes Presidential Center, University of Louisville Ekstrom Library Photographic Archives and W.H. Bass Photo Co., Inc.

Thanks to the four individuals who reviewed the final text for accuracy, Eric Bronsky, David Schafer, Shelden S. King and Douglas Preston. A special thanks goes to Jim McFarlane who reviewed the preliminary proof and assisted the author in getting several questions answered.

To benefit future historians who attempt additional research in this area, we have included several notes on subjects that are not necessarily appropriate in the basic text as well as a detailed bibliography. These items will be found at the end of the book.

Larry Plachno
Polo, Illinois
April 29, 1988

Cleveland, Southwestern & Columbus car 128 makes a passenger stop in Berlin Heights, Ohio headed east to Cleveland. Berlin Heights, a small town located a few miles east of Norwalk, was unusual in being served by two major interurban lines. The Cleveland-Norwalk lines of both the CSW&C and the Lake Shore Electric passed through the town and then crossed each other just southwest of the community. DAVID SCHAFER COLLECTION.

Utica in 1910

Utica, New York was brimming with optimism in the spring of 1910 when the Utica Boosters set off on their history-making 2,000-mile journey by interurban electric railway. Begun as a humble frontier trading post right after the close of the American Revolution, Utica was incorporated as a village in 1798 and as a city in 1832. Located at the western end of the historic Mohawk Valley, Utica was well situated, both on the main transportation route between the Atlantic seaboard and the Great Lakes, and at the gateway to both western New York and the Adirondack Mountains to the north.

In 1910, the Oneida Railway and the Utica & Mohawk Valley interurban lines were just the latest additions to Utica's impressive array of transportation facilities. These included the Erie Canal, highways (such as they were at that time), and an extensive street railway system. Both the New York Central & Hudson River Railroad's "water level route" main line and the parallel West Shore line passed through the city and it was also the junction point for two Central branches to the north. Branches of two anthracite railroads — the Delaware, Lackawanna & Western and the New York, Ontario & Western — also reached Utica from the south.

Utica already had a long history of innovation in transportation and communication. It was a terminus of the first section of the Erie Canal opened to traffic (Utica to Rome, in 1819) and of New York state's first long-distance railroad (the Utica & Schenectady, completed in 1836). Utica businessmen organized the first commercial application of Morse's telegraph in the 1840s, which led in turn to the formation of the nation's first wire service for news. John Butterfield of Utica organized the Butterfield Overland Mail stagecoach line from Missouri to California in 1858, and in 1863 he also opened Utica's first horsecar line.

Uticans were also prominent in the political arena. In 1910, the Utica Boosters were proud of the fact that their friend and neighbor, former Mayor and former Congressman James Schoolcraft Sherman, was serving as vice president of the United States under William Howard Taft. For a time right after the Civil War, both of New York's United States Senators were from Utica, Roscoe Conkling and Francis Kernan. Horatio Seymour of Utica served two terms as governor of New York before losing the presidency (some would say, unfortunately) to General Ulysses S. Grant in 1868.

Wherever they looked in 1910, Uticans could see signs of growth and prosperity. New buildings were rising on every hand. Just since about 1900, such landmarks as the Savings Bank of Utica and the City National Bank, Fraser's and John A. Roberts' department stores, Utica Free Academy (high school) and the Utica Public Library, the Masonic Temple, the Labor Temple, and clubhouses for the Fort Schuyler Club (for men) and the New Century Club (for women) had been added to the local scene. Already under construction or on the drawing boards were a new Central Fire Station, a million-dollar Oneida County Courthouse, a ten-story Hotel Utica and (probably of special interest to trip organizer C. Loomis Allen) a magnificent new Union Station which would include office space for New York State Railways, a subsidiary of the New York Central & Hudson River.

Manufacturing was booming as well. Textile mills were a mainstay of the local economy and at the turn of the century Utica proclaimed itself "the knit-goods capital of the world." Trolley pilgrim Arthur Hind operated a huge factory in nearby Clark Mills that made plush upholstery fabric. But the city's name was carried abroad on more than just union suits (invented in Utica) and sheets. Utica was also home to manufacturers of everything from furnaces and bedsprings to agricultural implements and fire extinguishers. At least one Utican was getting in on the ground floor of the automobile age; Charles S. Mott — who would later become a founder of General Motors (and a billionaire in the process) — got his start here, making wheels and axles. The Savage Arms Company was earning a world-wide reputation for its rifles and pistols. Never missing an opportunity for publicity, Savage supplied each man on the trip with a watch fob in the shape of one of its automatic pistols.

Utica's population was growing by leaps and bounds. From just under 3,000 in 1820 (the first census in which Utica was enumerated as a separate town), it had swelled to 22,524 in 1860, 33,914 in 1880, and

This circa 1900-1905 photo looks "down" (north) on Utica's Genesee Street during the era immediately prior to the arrival of the third rail interurban cars of Oneida Railway. The large structure in the center of the photo is the Mann Building while Bagg's Hotel is the darker building at the end of the street. The two local streetcars had little competition from automobiles at this early date. ONEIDA COUNTY HISTORICAL SOCIETY.

This early postcard view looks south on Genesee Street from the bridge over the Erie Canal and shows some of Utica's downtown commercial activity. An interurban car of the Oneida Railway passes a local streetcar in the center of the photo. ONEIDA COUNTY HISTORICAL SOCIETY.

56,383 in 1900. The 1910 census would show another increase of nearly one-third, to 74,419. The original Yankee pioneers from New England had long since been joined by throngs of Welsh, German and Irish immigrants and these "old" immigrants from northern and western Europe were rapidly being outnumbered by thousands more Italians, Poles, Jews, Syrians, Lebanese and other "new" immigrants from southern and eastern Europe and the Levant. Perhaps not all of the Utica Boosters welcomed these newcomers with open arms, but in the cities they visited they did take note of the local ethnic neighborhoods, housing conditions and the like, all of which had relevance to Utica.

Nor were the amenities being overlooked either during this, "the City Beautiful" period of urban planning. In 1910, Utica was undergoing a transformation and beautification that included the elimination of railroad grade crossings and the development of an extensive system of parks and parkways. Financed by local philanthropist Thomas R. Proctor and planned by the prestigious landscape architectural firm of Olmsted Brothers of Brookline, Massachusetts, Utica was being ringed with a "green belt" that remains one of its choicest assets to this day. Work was also under way to remove the old Erie Canal (with its many bridges) and the Mohawk River (with its spring floods) from downtown Utica and to replace them with a new Barge Canal and straightened channel, respectively. Public works projects such as these were of special interest to the trolley pilgrims in many of the cities they visited.

In the decades since 1910, Utica has undergone many changes. The textile mills have all but vanished, replaced by durable goods manufacturers, high-technology research and development, military contractors and such service businesses as insurance companies, bank offices, three colleges, a state prison and hospitals. Some of the proud new buildings going up in 1910 are now considered old landmarks, while others have fallen to the wrecker's ball to make way for new high-rises (or for parking lots and garages). Bagg's Hotel, from which the trolley pilgrims embarked, was torn down in 1932.

The last trolley left the streets of Utica in 1941, but the old Main Street carbarn continued to serve Utica Transit buses until 1979. Replaced by a new garage on another site, the barn was razed to provide improved access and parking for the restored Union Station.

Nearly all of the West Shore tracks over which the third rail cars sped between Utica and Syracuse were abandoned piecemeal in the 1970s by Penn Central and later Conrail. Locally, only a tiny segment of the West Shore mainline remains intact, serving to connect former DL&W and NYO&W trackage, all operated today by the Delaware-Otsego System. Several miles west of Utica, between Vernon and Sherrill, a well-preserved brick substation stands as a silent reminder of the all-too-brief heyday of the Third Rail.

Uticans of today — indeed residents of any community seeking to improve itself — could profit by the story of the Utica Boosters and *The Longest Interurban Charter*. While it may no longer be possible to duplicate this trip "under the singing trolley wire" the lesson of learning from others' examples remains valid. On behalf of all who live in or near the Utica of today, I wish to thank Larry Plachno for undertaking to retell the full story of this colorful episode in our city's history.

Douglas M. Preston
Director
Oneida County Historical Society

This early postcard view shows an interurban car and a local streetcar passing the Olbliston Apartments on upper Genesee Street in Utica. The building still stands but the electric cars have long since been replaced by automobiles. ONEIDA COUNTY HISTORICAL SOCIETY.

1

The Interurban Network

The electric interurban railways were a natural outgrowth of the municipal streetcar. In the 1880s virtually all municipal public transportation was provided by horsecars or cable cars. By 1888, the electric streetcar had been perfected to the point where it was accepted for commercial use. Within the next decade, the electric streetcar became the most popular method for providing municipal public transportation.

It was inevitable that the concept of extending the streetcar lines beyond municipal limits would emerge. These lines operated with heavier cars and either connected rural areas to the city or connected neighboring cities. They eventually were called interurban electric railways. The steam railroads had mixed emotions over this new industry that was taking away their local business. Some steam railroads fought the interurbans at every opportunity and often refused permission to cross their tracks. Other steam railroads were philosophical about the loss of marginal local business and either worked with or owned interurban lines.

From 1900 to 1910, there was a massive boom in building interurban railways. The great majority were concentrated in the Midwest but many lines were built in the eastern and western states. Virtually without exception, the typical interurban was a local enterprise. Some companies were only a few miles long and only rarely did a single company build more than 100 miles of track. However, many companies were involved in later mergers that attempted to join several smaller companies together in order to connect major cities. The convenient and frequent schedules, provided on generally unsophisticated trackage and right-of-way, made the interurbans very suitable for providing local service but poorly situated for providing long distance service.

On February 4, 1910, the Winona Interurban Railway linked Goshen and Peru, Indiana, thus completing a network of Midwest interurban lines. It was then possible for a passenger to ride by interurban from Little Falls or Oneonta, New York to Elkhart Lake, Wisconsin. Oneonta was a greater distance than Little Falls, but Little Falls was generally considered the end of the interurban network because it provided steam railroad connections for continuing on to New York City. However, such an interurban trip would have been highly impractical since it was slow and required numerous changes between the cars of different companies. Moreover, the route was technically incomplete, at least initially, and required walking across one gap in Rochester, New York and the use of steam power and a rapid transit train in Chicago.

It can be argued that the Midwest interurban network was not so much a network as a conglomeration of individual companies. Each company had been constructed individually to somewhat different specifications and often without regard to the ability to interchange equipment with other lines. Most interurbans used standard railroad gauge (4 feet, 8½ inches) track, although many lines in Pennsylvania, Cincinnati and Louisville had different gauges. Some insisted on steam railroad standards for right-of-way, grades and curves but most accepted sharp curves and operated on local streetcar tracks in larger communities. Most used an overhead trolley wire for electric current, but the height of the wire above the rails varied somewhat and some interurbans used a third rail. Most interurbans used electric power at about 600 volts direct current but some used other voltages or even alternating current. There were also variations in coupler design and clearance restrictions.

Due to the local nature of patronage and the differences between the companies, long distance operation of interurban passenger cars was a rarity. On longer trips it was simply easier and faster to go by steam railroad.

Some connecting lines did develop joint service with pooled equipment in order to provide through service

---

PRECEDING PAGE

The center of interurban activities in 1910 was the Indianapolis Traction Terminal. Opened in 1904, the terminal featured a trainshed covering nine tracks. The adjacent nine-story building contained ticket offices, a waiting room and retail stores with offices on the upper floors for interurban companies and the industry trade association. This photo is from the 1910 era. W.H. BASS PHOTO CO.

The Longest Interurban Charter • 13

In a typical interurban scene, a Sandusky, Norwalk & Mansfield car trundles down unpaved Sandusky Street in Plymouth, Ohio prior to 1910. DAVID SCHAFER COLLECTION.

Many of the Midwest interurban lines experienced difficulty in obtaining permission to cross steam railroad tracks. Many such situations were resolved only after a pitched battle between interurban and steam railroad track gangs followed by a court order. Even when the steam line evidenced no hostility, the interurban line was usually the junior partner at the crossing and responsible for most or all of the construction and maintenance expense. This shows the substantial and possibly overly-elaborate interlocker that was built to protect the crossing of the Lake Shore Electric and the Lake Shore & Michigan Southern at Fremont, Ohio. The photo was taken on July 14, 1919. This interlocking plant is now but a memory since both railroads have long since ripped up their tracks. DAVE McLELLAN COLLECTION.

14 • *The Longest Interurban Charter*

Freight or express motors were the interurban equivalent of a powered box car and some were powerful enough to pull one or two non-powered or "trailer" cars. Lake Shore Electric 41 was built in 1905 by the Niles Car Co. Cars like this regularly ran the daily 340-mile freight trip from Cleveland to Cincinnati. CHARLES E. FROHMAN COLLECTION / HAYES PRESIDENTIAL CENTER.

between major cities. Good examples are Indianapolis-Dayton, Indianapolis-Fort Wayne and Indianapolis-Louisville. Each of these routes was eventually consolidated under a single management. Service was a special situation between Indianapolis and Louisville since one intermediate section of track at a higher voltage limited the use of through cars. Long east-west links between Indiana and Ohio were tried but were not generally successful. In only a very few cases were interurban passenger cars regularly scheduled for trips of over 200 miles. A 247-mile run between Indianapolis and Zanesville, Ohio operated briefly just prior to World War I. The longest scheduled passenger interurban run was the 277-mile trip from Cincinnati to Detroit. It lasted only two years in the early 1930s.

It might be noted that the interurbans eventually found more of a need to pool long distance trains for freight and package express than for passengers. This became particularly true by the 1920s when revenue from package express and freight was growing and compensating for declining passenger revenue. Interurban freight traditionally ran at night when the tracks were free of passenger trains. Express motors connected major interurban centers with nightly trips. Many pulled one or more non-powered trailers that were the interurban equivalent of box cars. Non-powered freight cars roamed freely throughout the interurban network while the powered express motors were occasionally pooled on runs covering two or more companies. The longest nightly freight run connected Cincinnati and Cleveland (approximately 340 miles) in 12 hours and technically ran over the tracks of five different companies. Beginning in 1929, this service lasted until May of 1937.

Long distance passenger charter movements over interurban lines were unusual. There were, however, some situations conducive to relatively regular charter operation over an adjoining line because of special attractions. For example, the Buffalo, Lockport & Rochester Railway ran charter trips to Niagara Falls over the International Railway. But overnight interurban charters were rare.

The 2,000-mile interurban trip covered by this book set the record for the longest interurban charter trip of all time. It was unique because the distance was totally out of character with typical interurban trips. It took a special reason and purpose to make such a trip by interurban practical. This trip was also unique from the standpoint of trackage covered. The fact that

Norwalk, Ohio was served by three different interurban lines: the Lake Shore Electric, the Cleveland, Southwestern & Columbus and the Sandusky, Norwalk & Mansfield. This photo of Norwalk's West Main Street shows a local centennial celebration in progress on July 19, 1909, and an interurban car approaching in the distance. Most interurban lines operated on city streets in larger communities. DAVID SCHAFER COLLECTION.

Most interurban lines did not have the financial backing to construct major bridges and structures. Unusual because of its size was the Lorain Road/Rocky River Bridge of the Cleveland, Southwestern & Columbus near Rockport, Ohio. DAVID SCHAFER COLLECTION.

16 • *The Longest Interurban Charter*

a single car was able to successfully operate over the rails of 28 different lines gave the interurban industry a new image of compatibility. It also suggests that the individuals and equipment involved deserve a great deal of credit.

One contemporary newspaper, when reporting this trip in 1910, prophetically commented: "There will be in a few years a line of street railways extending from coast to coast . . . The present generation will live to see trolley trips from the Atlantic to the Pacific as a common thing."[1] Unfortunately, that prediction was wide of the mark. Except for a few major lines in the western states, there was no significant expansion of the interurban industry after 1910. The Midwest network of connected interurban lines had essentially reached its major extent by that time.

By 1915, the automobile had emerged as a serious threat to the local patronage of the interurbans. By 1920, several of the interurbans were in financial trouble due to loss of ridership to automobiles. By 1925, some of the weaker companies had given up and abandoned their lines. Many of the remaining lines failed to survive the Depression of the 1930s. Virtually nothing was left of the Midwest interurban network by the start of World War II.

However, this review of the Utica interurban charter of 1910 gives us an opportunity to view the interurban network in its prime and to "ride along" on a trip that was unique and interesting.

The Winona Interurban Railway was one of the more unique members of the interurban network. Best known as the connecting link between the Indiana/Ohio lines (at Peru, Indiana) and the Northern Indiana/Chicago lines (at Goshen, Indiana), the Winona refused to run on Sundays in its early years for religious reasons and operated two of these striking 1910 "windsplitter" cars from the Jewett Car Company. The Winona was a good example of pooled service with adjacent lines. Regular service operated from Peru to Michigan City, Indiana in conjunction with the Northern Indiana Railway and from Goshen to Indianapolis in conjunction with the Indiana Union Traction Company. Although the company tried, Winona was unable to obtain cooperation on a proposed pooled service from South Bend to Indianapolis. W.H. BASS PHOTO CO.

2

Planning and Preparations

According to reports published nearly 40 years later, credit for suggesting this tour goes to C. Loomis Allen. Allen, vice president and general manager of the interurban lines operating out of Utica, New York, and quiescent member of the Utica Chamber of Commerce, made the suggestion for the trip to the Utica Chamber of Commerce in early 1910. Allen conceived the idea of a tour to demonstrate the rapidity with which electric transportation was being developed.

Exact dates are unclear, but it appears that Mr. Allen started thinking about the trip and making contacts regarding its possibility as early as December of 1909. Based on materials published in the trade press, Allen had a proposed itinerary worked out by February of 1910.

By way of background, it should be noted that some of the important links that made this trip possible were not completed until 1907 and 1908. For example, the Norwalk-Shelby line and the through link between Indianapolis and Louisville were not completed until 1907. This same year saw the opening of the third rail Oneida Railway between Utica and Syracuse. The following year saw the completion of the Bucyrus-Marion line (thus linking Cleveland and Columbus), the Rochester-Lockport line, and the Syracuse-Rochester line (via Auburn). The final link (other than the 80 feet missing on the west side of Rochester, which figures prominently in this story) was closed in January of 1909 when the Buffalo & Lake Erie Traction reached Buffalo. Hence, the trip contemplated by Allen was technically possible after this date.

Two things happened in late 1909 that were significant. November saw the Buffalo & Lake Erie Traction begin through service between Buffalo and Erie. December of that year saw the Rochester, Syracuse & Eastern put its new line in operation that shortened the distance between Syracuse and Rochester by eliminating the jog to Auburn. It is believed that these two incidents prompted Allen to contemplate the possibility of a long distance charter from Utica.

As initially proposed, the concept was that prominent Utica businessmen would visit several Midwestern cities. One purpose was to investigate what other cities were doing along civic lines and with public utilities that might be of value to Utica. A second purpose was to look for business opportunities that could be used in Utica. A third purpose was to find ideas that Utica could use to encourage conventions and entice new business to locate in the community.

In retrospect, the use of an interurban car was a sound and practical idea for this particular trip. Motor vehicles and roads were still somewhat primitive in 1910 and would not have been practical. Travel by steam railroad would have worked, but an interurban car was much more flexible.

The Utica Chamber of Commerce was cool to the idea, but the Utica Boosters were strongly in favor of such a trip. A general committee was soon established to plan the trip. Included on the committee were William T. Baker, chairman; Tom W. Johnson, vice chairman; F.W. Bensberg, treasurer; and J. Soley Cole, secretary. Subcommittees were then established for various activities. C. Loomis Allen was to arrange for transportation and determine where the group was going. Tom W. Johnson, the manager of Bagg's Hotel, was to arrange for overnight hotel accommodations based on Allen's proposed schedule. J. Soley Cole, the secretary of the Utica Chamber of Commerce, was to get in touch with the Chambers of Commerce along the route, inform them of the proposed schedule and request their assistance. The Utica group's desire "to learn instead of teach and preach" ensured a favorable welcome along the way.

Planning The Route

In 1910, the New York Central & Hudson River Railroad held a majority stock interest control of four interurban lines and all street railway operations in the

PRECEDING PAGE

This photo of the interior of car 502 was taken after it was converted for the Utica Electric Railway Tour. The photo looks towards the front of the car and shows several of the individual willow arm chairs and a few carefully placed brass spittoons. ZINTMASTER / ONEIDA COUNTY HISTORICAL SOCIETY.

First Itinerary and Final Itinerary

It is unfortunate that no copy of Allen's detailed itinerary appears to have survived these 78 years. The closest things available are the following two items.

This first itinerary was published in the March 12, 1910, *Electric Railway Journal*. It was undoubtedly prepared by C. Loomis Allen and represents his preliminary itinerary. It is interesting because it shows both mileage and running time in detail. The total distance involved was 2049.82 miles and the expected running time was 81 hours and 48 minutes. It should be noted that several items on this preliminary itinerary were changed before the trip finally started. The final trip was expanded to 14 days, from the 13 shown here, Cleveland replaced Mansfield as an overnight stop and the projected side trip to Cincinnati was later eliminated.

First day, Utica to Rochester, 134.82 miles, 4 hours, 18 minutes. **Second day,** Rochester to Erie, Pa., 169 miles, 7 hours, 33 minutes. **Third day,** Erie, Pa., to Mansfield, Ohio, 202.50 miles, 9 hours, 46 minutes. **Fourth day,** Mansfield, Ohio, to Columbus, Ohio, 98 miles, 4 hours, 35 minutes. **Fifth day,** Columbus, Ohio, to Cincinnati, Ohio, 131 miles, 5 hours, 10 minutes. **Sixth day,** Cincinnati, Ohio, to Indianapolis, Ind., 163.66 miles, 6 hours, 53 minutes. **Seventh day,** Indianapolis, Ind., to Louisville, Ky., 117 miles, 4 hours. **Eighth day,** Louisville, Ky., to Fort Wayne, Ind., 251.50 miles, 8 hours, 40 minutes. **Ninth day,** Fort Wayne, Ind., to Toledo, Ohio, 148 miles, 5 hours, 22 minutes. **Tenth day,** Toledo, Ohio, to Detroit, Mich., 56 miles, 2 hours. **Eleventh day,** Detroit, Mich., to Cleveland, Ohio, 172 miles, 6 hours, 35 minutes. **Twelfth day,** Cleveland, Ohio, to Buffalo, 190.50 miles, 9 hours, 35 minutes. **Thirteenth day,** Buffalo to Utica, 215.82 miles, 7 hours, 21 minutes.

This map appeared in the March 12, 1910, *Electric Railway Journal* and was used to illustrate the accompanying itinerary. The round trip to Cincinnati was later eliminated. This map also showed a jog to Auburn between Syracuse and Rochester although the itinerary never mentioned this routing. J.R. McFARLANE COLLECTION.

The following itinerary was published in the *Utica Observer* on May 10, 1910, the day the tour departed. This information was taken from the booklet handed out to the passengers and their families that morning. As such this was the final itinerary and controlled operations during the tour.

First Day: May 10, leave Utica 10:30 a.m. Arrive Syracuse 11:55 a.m. Luncheon. Leave Syracuse 3 p.m. Arrive Rochester 5:50 p.m. Headquarters, Hotel Seneca.

Second Day: May 11, leave Rochester 9 a.m. Arrive Buffalo 12:03 p.m. Luncheon at Hotel Lafayette. Leave Buffalo 1:30 p.m. Arrive Erie, Pa. 6 p.m. Headquarters, Reed House.

Third Day: May 12, leave Erie 10 a.m. Arrive Ashtabula 12:40 p.m. Luncheon. Leave Ashtabula 1:30 p.m. Arrive Cleveland 3:55 p.m. Headquarters, Hotel Hollenden.

Fourth Day: May 13, leave Cleveland 9 a.m. Luncheon en route. Arrive Columbus 6:16 p.m. Headquarters, Hotel Chittenden.

Fifth Day: May 14, leave Columbus 7 a.m. Arrive Dayton 9:15 a.m. Headquarters, Hotel Algonquin.

Sixth Day: May 15, leave Dayton 3 p.m. Arrive Indianapolis 6:58 p.m. Headquarters, Hotel Claypool.

Seventh Day: May 16, leave Indianapolis 8 a.m. Arrive Louisville 12 noon. Headquarters, Hotel Seelbach.

Eighth Day: May 17, leave Louisville 2 p.m. Arrive Indianapolis 6 p.m. Headquarters, Hotel Claypool.

Ninth Day: May 18, leave Indianapolis 10 a.m. Arrive Kokomo 12 noon. Luncheon. Leave Kokomo 1:30 p.m. Arrive Fort Wayne 4:10 p.m. Headquarters, Hotel Anthony.

Tenth Day: May 19, leave Fort Wayne 10:30 a.m. Arrive Lima, Ohio 12:40 p.m. Luncheon. Leave Lima 3 p.m. Arrive Toledo 6:12 p.m. Headquarters, Hotel Secor.

Eleventh Day: May 20, leave Toledo 10:30 a.m. Arrive Detroit 12:30 p.m. Headquarters, Hotel Pontchartrain.

Twelfth Day: May 21, leave Detroit 10 a.m. Arrive Fremont 1:10 p.m. Luncheon. Leave Fremont 2:30 p.m. Arrive Cleveland 5:55 p.m. Headquarters, Hotel Hollenden.

Thirteenth Day: May 22, leave Cleveland 8 a.m. Arrive Erie 1:05 p.m. Luncheon. Leave Erie 2 p.m. Arrive Buffalo 6 p.m. Headquarters, Hotel Lafayette.

Fourteenth Day: May 23, leave Buffalo 9 a.m. Arrive Rochester 12:03 p.m. Luncheon. Leave Rochester 1:30 p.m. Arrive Syracuse 4:20 p.m. Leave Syracuse 4:30 p.m. Arrive Utica 5:58 p.m.

Utica and Syracuse were officially connected by interurban on June 15, 1907, when this special train carried officials and special guests. C. Loomis Allen was the motorman of this special train which consisted of cars 502 (leading) and 504. Regular service began the following day. MANNING / ONEIDA COUNTY HISTORICAL SOCIETY.

Rochester-Syracuse-Utica area. During the previous year, the two Rochester interurbans (to Geneva and to Sodus Point) and the Rochester City Lines had been consolidated into a new company, the New York State Railways. This new company was still controlled by NYC&HR and its interest in the Syracuse Rapid Transit Railway, the Oneida Railway and the Utica & Mohawk Valley Railway were turned over to New York State Railways. However, the Syracuse, Oneida and Utica properties were operated independently under C. Loomis Allen, vice president and general manager of each company. Mr. Allen was also a vice president of New York State Railways.

The Oneida Railway operated a third rail interurban line between Utica and Syracuse over West Shore Railroad (NYC&HR) tracks. The Utica & Mohawk Valley Railway ran between Rome, Utica and Little Falls, New York and included city and suburban car operation in Rome and Utica.

Allen appears to have been a "hands on" type of manager and was generally to be found at the scene of any important or unusual activity. On Tuesday, May 21, 1907, he performed as the motorman on an inspection trip for company officers over the newly-completed Oneida Railway. On June 15, 1907, Allen acted as the motorman on the first official run on the Oneida Railway with cars 502-504. And, of course, he was deeply involved in all facets of the forthcoming "Utica Electric Railway Tour."

Once the trip concept was approved, Allen developed very extensive plans that covered much of the Midwest by interurban electric railway involving approximately 2,000 miles in two weeks of travel. Along with his general passenger agent, C.R. Gowen, Allen contacted all interurban and city lines along the proposed route. He not only had to secure permission for a chartered interurban car to operate on their tracks but also had to arrange for a "pilot" as well as for car storage and service.

In addition, circulars were provided by T.C. Cherry, U&MV superintendent, to the various lines giving the dimensions of the car to be used on the charter. The companies were requested to provide information on any modifications necessary to make the car adaptable to their trackage and the trackage of the cities to be visited. Only two mechanical changes were subsequently made to the car.

The general plan anticipated that a pilot or crew would come on board while operating on each foreign road to guide the car's Oneida Railway crew. On virtually all lines the car would operate as an "extra" under its own power. Actual running would be confined to daylight hours and the passengers would spend their nights in hotels along the way. Stops were also planned for meals and sightseeing.

Contemporary reports indicate that Allen drew up a very detailed itinerary that actually scheduled arrivals and departures to the minute. The schedule called for the car to average 38 miles per hour while underway. It also permitted the interurban lines and groups along the way to plan for the car's arrival.

The electric railway industry was first made aware of the trip through a short notice in the March 5, 1910, issue of *Electric Railway Journal*. Undoubtedly placed by Allen, this sketchy paragraph mentioned some of the cities to be visited, suggested a proposed departure date of "about May 1, 1910," and indicated that two private cars would be used.

A week later, a half-page article on the proposed trip appeared in the *Electric Railway Journal* of March 12, 1910. This time, a map of the route was offered as well as an unusually detailed itinerary that included running time between cities in minutes, and mileage to two decimal places. This article talked about using more

Official builders photo from the J.G. Brill Company shows the interior of Oneida Railway car 512 when completed in 1907. Car 502 would have had a similar interior. This view looks towards the front of the car; the rest room and water fountain are on the left. Compare with the photo on page 18. J.R. McFARLANE COLLECTION.

Taken at the same time as the above, this is the official J.G. Brill builder's photo of car 512. Note that the trolley poles and third rail shoes had not yet been affixed to the car. M.D. McCARTER COLLECTION.

than one car and gave a departure date of "before May 3, 1910."

This early proposed itinerary is interesting because it showed a side trip from Dayton to Cincinnati and return. The Cincinnati trip was later eliminated and the group remained in Dayton for a longer time. The revised, final itinerary was printed in booklet form and made available to passengers and interested individuals.

It is unfortunate that a copy of Allen's schedule failed to survive intact. In numerous locations, individuals or groups were able to meet or see the car because they knew the schedule. Based on what is known of the original schedule, it appears that the group started off each morning on time and with good intentions. However, on several occasions they fell behind their schedule during the day, sometimes by several hours. On most occasions this was not the fault of the proposed schedule or operating conditions but rather the group frequently elected to make additional stops, stay late at a stop or take an unscheduled tour. These sudden changes in plans were apparently accommodated without complaint by the interurban lines being covered.

Much of the success of the trip was due to Allen's thorough planning. The operations and mechanics of the trip could hardly have gone better. There were no major problems (and few minor ones) even though the chartered car was hundreds of miles from home and on foreign rails. Allen was well known and admired in the interurban industry because the car was frequently met by officers and managers of the interurban lines who rode along or served as pilots. It also appears that many of the interurban lines declined to charge the group for electric power, track usage and other services.

Reservations and Meetings Along the Way

Hotel reservations and planning were handled by Tom W. Johnson, who was the manager of Bagg's Hotel in Utica and also president of the company building the new Hotel Utica, identified as "one of the Utica landlords." He also went on the trip to handle hotel arrangements, leaving the travelers free to "enjoy themselves and absorb knowledge." Each passenger's luggage would be confined to one suitcase and a tag with the owner's name was provided. A special compartment in the electric car was provided for storage, and hotel trucks would handle baggage between the car and the hotels.

J. Soley Cole, the secretary of the Utica Chamber of Commerce, had the responsibility of sending letters to business organizations of the cities to be visited. This aspect of the trip also went well because of these prior arrangements. Groups and individuals were waiting at all major points and several minor ones along the way. Most had arranged tours, luncheons, dinners or other activities for the Utica group.

The Chartered Car

C. Loomis Allen selected car 502 of the Oneida Railway Company for the trip. Built by the J.G. Brill Company in Philadelphia in early 1907, 502 was one of 15 wood single-end cars that started service on Oneida Railway when it opened. The car weighed approximately 78,000 pounds, was 49 feet long, 8½ feet wide, and had a height of 13 feet, 8 inches. It was equipped with four General Electric motors that permitted relatively high speeds on 600 volt direct current. It also had multiple unit control and trains of three or four cars were not uncommon on the Oneida line.

The car was equipped for under-running third rail power collection while running on the electrified West Shore Railroad between Syracuse and Utica. It also had trolley poles which were used for operating on the street railway trackage in Utica, Oneida and Syracuse. On this special trip the trolley poles would be used for virtually the entire distance.

In normal operation the car seated 52 passengers in two compartments — smoking and non-smoking. It had mahogany woodwork and electric incandescent lights in ground glass globes. Plate glass passenger windows were below semi-circular "fan windows" made of leaded art glass. The exterior was painted a standard Pullman green. At this time the car was valued at $13,000.

After being selected, car 502 was run through the shops and extensively refurbished for the trip.

There were only two mechanical changes made to the car at this time. The height of the front pilot was raised about five inches. In addition, new steel wheels were fitted with a tread of 3½ inches, replacing the old wheels with a tread of four inches. These adjustments were necessary so that the car would operate properly on the tracks of the other interurban and streetcar lines it would encounter.

The regular seats were removed and the car was thoroughly cleaned. Next, a carpet of rich, mossy green color was placed on the floor. Seating for the passengers was provided with 25 willow arm chairs. The chairs had cushions and were not fastened to the floor so that they could be placed in any position. In addition, a dozen camp chairs were provided for use in entertaining guests. They came in very handy on the trip as both individuals and small groups boarded or rode on the car on many occasions.

Other special equipment was also installed including spittoons, some type of early refrigerator or ice box and a water cooler. The rest room, in the rear of the car adjacent to the oval window, was retained. Both sides of the car were lettered "Utica, N.Y., Electric Railway Tour" in gold leaf over the regular Pullman green exterior.

Just before departure, Tom W. Johnson stocked the car from the Bagg's Hotel wine cellar. It reportedly carried refreshments "to satisfy the most diversified and discriminating tastes." Later notes indicated that the average daily consumption per passenger during the trip was 1½ drinks. One suspects this applied to the initial stock only and not the additional supplies brought on board during the trip.

The Crew

A crew was hand-picked for the special trip. John O'Hara was selected as conductor while George Moore was selected as motorman. Both had been with the Oneida Railway since it started operations three years previously. They were selected because of seniority as

This photo shows three of the "500" series Oneida Railway cars when brand new in 1907. Car 504 leads the train. Note the unusual under running third rail used by the company. J.R. McFARLANE COLLECTION.

C. Loomis Allen picked the two crew members for the Utica Electric Railway Tour. Conductor John O'Hara is shown on the left and Motorman George Moore is on the right. Both had worked for Oneida Railway since it opened in 1907. The original photos were taken by Zintmaster of Utica and were reproduced from a 1910 Utica newspaper. ONEIDA COUNTY HISTORICAL SOCIETY.

These souvenir baggage tags were given to the participants of the Utica Electric Railway Tour. In May of 1910 the Hotel Utica was still in the planning stage or early phase of construction and did not open until 1912. Hence, these tags could be considered advance publicity. ONEIDA COUNTY HISTORICAL SOCIETY.

well as past performance. In addition to operating the car, the crew would also be responsible for taking the car to an appropriate carbarn or yard for the night and for some of the car cleaning and servicing on the tour.

The third member of the crew was William Jackson, who was the porter for the group. Jackson was considered one of the best-trained waiters at Bagg's Hotel. His services were provided by Tom W. Johnson without charge to the group. Jackson became a favorite of the passengers and received several gifts for his attentive service. He was supplied with a spick-and-span blue uniform and a cap with gold letters reading "Utica Electric Trip." He also was given a white coat for special occasions.

In addition to the three-man crew, three railway officials were responsible for the day-to-day operation of the trip and at least one was on board at all times. Expectedly, General Manager C. Loomis Allen went along for most of the trip to supervise operations. Superintendent T.C. Cherry was Allen's assistant on the trip and took over when Allen was not on board. Edward J. Wright, superintendent of Oneida Railway, also supervised the return portion of the trip from Detroit back to Utica.

At this time, Mr. Cherry was the superintendent of the Utica & Mohawk Valley Railway. In later years his stature would increase substantially. Talmadge C. Cherry left Utica in 1912 for management positions on Schenectady Railway and later Maryland Electric Railways. In 1916, he returned to Syracuse, his birthplace, and became general manager of the various segments of the Beebe Syndicate lines as they were being individually reorganized. He was thus identified with the Auburn & Syracuse Electric R.R., Empire State R.R., Rochester & Syracuse R.R. and Syracuse Northern Electric Ry. through their good years of the 1920s, their decline and abandonment in 1930-32, and their final dissolution by 1935. Mr. Cherry died in 1941 at age 65.

Participants

The trip was announced as early as four months in advance. The Utica Boosters and the Chamber of Commerce were heavily involved and the trip was widely discussed by Utica businessmen. Participation was open to all members of the Utica Chamber of Commerce but particular emphasis was placed on getting any local Utica business man involved, regardless of chamber membership.

Financially, the trip was set up independent of any organization or company. Each of the participants would contribute an equal share of the total expenses. The resulting fund would be used to cover expenses including the chartered car, fees from other interurban lines, some of the meals, and all of the hotel rooms and baggage handling. A final accounting would be made at the end of the trip. As things turned out, each participant paid about $110 for a seat on the trip.

A total of 21 businessmen are confirmed as having participated in the trip, all but one from Utica or the Utica area. They were described as "the leading businessmen and citizens of Utica." Included were the following:[1]

Jacob Agne . . . . Architect and President of the Herald-Dispatch Publishing Co.
W. Fred Allen . . . . Stone Contractor and Manufacturer
Frank J. Baker . . . . President of the Utica Common Council and Florist
Charles E. Barnard . . . . Retired Merchant and Capitalist
Edwin T. Batsford . . . . Retired Manufacturer
F. William Bensberg . . . . Utica Park Commissioner and Treasurer of trip
William L. Brock . . . . Capitalist
Fred A. Cassidy . . . . Undertaker
Wilbur S. Clark . . . . Storage and Transfer Business
J. Soley Cole . . . Secretary of the Utica Chamber of Commerce and former Newspaper Man
Charles Y. Fuller . . . . Capitalist and Contractor
Dr. Clement T. Guillaume . . . . Medical Doctor
Arthur Hind . . . . Plush Manufacturer
Tom W. Johnson . . . . Manager of Bagg's Hotel and Chairman of Trip Tour Committee
Henry M. Love . . . . Attorney
John L. Maher . . . . Clothing Merchant and Manufacturer
Fred McLean . . . . Dyer
William Schachtel . . . . . Representative of the Utica Press
Fred W. Sessions . . . . Wholesale and Retail Milliner
B. Allen Whiffen . . . . Meat Distributor
Charles L. Williams . . . . . . Fish and Poultry Dealer

The original "sign up" for the trip included 20 individuals; all of the above other than Fred McLean. Three others signed up to join the group prior to departure. Fred McLean joined the group at a late date and he did board the trip in Utica to become the twenty-first member of the group. Fred E. Payne of Clinton was a late addition to the group. He did ride on the May 9 trip to Little Falls but failed to join the group as planned on the morning of May 10. Mr. S.H. French was a late addition to the group who was due to board at Rochester. He did not join the group and nothing more was mentioned about the man. Hence, as many as 23 men were signed up for the tour prior to departure, but only 21 are actually confirmed as having been on board.

Bill Schachtel, known as "Schack" among his friends, was responsible for most of the documentation of the trip. Every day he sat down to record the daily occurrences of what transpired. These were mailed back to the *Utica Press* and were published daily as the trip progressed. Some of the daily accounts of activities covered more than two columns in the newspaper.

William L. Brock came from Toronto to ride the trip and is the only passenger known to have come from outside the Utica area. It is possible that Brock's involvement with the trip was connected with Canadian financing of the Buffalo, Lockport & Rochester Railway.

Even before starting, the group was given different names by various newspapers. Initially, they were formally called the "Utica Electric Railway Tour." As time went on this was shortened to the "Utica Business Men" or simply the "Utica Group." On several occasions the group was appropriately called "The Trolley Pilgrims."

Oneida Railway car 520 is shown boarding passengers at Clinton Square in Syracuse prior to running as a limited to Utica. This shows the original appearance of the "500" series Oneida Railway cars with single end operation and end train doors. M.D. McCARTER COLLECTION.

Two Oneida Railway third rail trains pass at the upper level of the Oneida Castle Union Station. This was the major station on the Oneida Railway between Utica and Syracuse. Ontario & Western steam trains crossed under the third rail tracks at this point and stopped at the lower level of this station. During the summer months as many as 5,000 passengers would transfer from the third rail to the steam trains in a single day in order to ride to Sylvan Beach on Oneida Lake. SHELDEN S. KING COLLECTION.

26 • *The Longest Interurban Charter*

A four-car train operates over the Utica & Mohawk Valley Line in about 1916. Although under the same management as the Oneida Railway, the U&MV had lighter cars and operated from an overhead trolley wire. J.R. McFARLANE COLLECTION.

The Track Gap in Rochester

At the time of planning the trip, the Oneida Railway was not physically connected with the Midwest interurban network as there was a small gap on the west side of Rochester. The Buffalo, Lockport and Rochester Railway was opened to Rochester in 1908 but the track ended on Lyell Avenue on the west side of town at the New York Central tracks at a point called Otis Station. Passengers walked 80 feet over the railroad crossing to where the Rochester City Lines track ended and where they could board a Lyell Avenue streetcar to ride to downtown Rochester.

It is known that general manager C. Loomis Allen was aware of this gap, but yet continued planning. This small but important gap was to play a significant part in the trip.

The Trial Trip and First Leg

On Monday, May 9, the day before the actual trip started, C. Loomis Allen decided to take car 502 on a trial trip for a last minute "shake down cruise." What made this trip particularly interesting is that Allen elected to go east over the Utica & Mohawk Valley to Little Falls rather than west over the Oneida Railway. It later became obvious that Allen was using Little Falls, New York (the accepted eastern end of the Midwest interurban network) as the official starting and ending point for the trip.

Boarding the car in Utica were General Manager C. Loomis Allen and T.C. Cherry, superintendent of the Utica & Mohawk Valley Railway. They were joined by Edward J. Wright, superintendent of the Oneida Railway; and Fred J. Baker, president of the Utica Common Council. F.W. Bensberg and Tom W. Johnson, both of whom were signed up for the trolley tour, managed to come along. In addition, William T. Johnson and Fred Payne of Clinton joined in the outing.

The car left Utica and headed east over the Utica & Mohawk Valley Line. At Mohawk, car 502 passed the connection with the Otsego & Herkimer Railroad (later the Southern New York Railway). Fifty-nine miles south via the O&H was Oneonta, New York, technically the most extreme point of the interurban network that stretched west to Wisconsin.

In Little Falls, the car was run to the Hotel Richmond. Evidentially, the trip had been announced in advance because a large group gathered to see car 502. The passengers on the car were entertained by Homer Snyder, J. Becker and the Smith Brothers.

The return to Utica was made quickly. Here the car ran south through Utica on Genesee Street to the West Shore Railroad tracks and was returned to the car barns at Utica Park (later Forest Park). Passengers on board commented that the car ran very smoothly.

C. Loomis Allen

The man who planned *The Longest Interurban Charter,* and who supervised much of its operation, was a nationally known leader in the field of electric railway engineering, management and finance. At one time or another he served as president of industry trade associations and had two honorary degrees conferred on him.

The earliest Allens came from Durham and Essex County, England and settled in the Syracuse, New York area. Chauncey Loomis Allen was born in Syracuse, New York on January 16, 1870, the son of George Richmond Allen and Mary Ann Brown Allen. He dropped the use of his first name at a relatively early age, replacing Chauncey with the initial C. Most of his friends called him Loomis.

Allen was educated in the common schools of Syracuse and the district school of Cicero in Onondaga County, New York. In March of 1886, at age 16, Allen entered Alfred University in Alfred, New York. He remained at Alfred University until June, 1889, and then attended Syracuse University during the fall term in 1889.

His first job started in February of 1890 with the engineering corps of the Norfolk & Western Railway Company. Allen worked on the surveying and construction of the Ohio Extension of the N&W and was successively employed as an axeman, chainman, rodman and inspector of masonry. This engagement lasted about two years, until February 15, 1892, when Allen returned to his hometown of Syracuse to engage in private practice as a civil engineer.

On April 15, 1892, Allen joined the engineering firm of Mather and Allen. This company was composed of Thomas H. Mather, Henry C. Allen, Theodore W. Clark and C. Loomis Allen. This firm engaged in the engineering of local improvements including sewers, sidewalks and both brick and asphalt street pavements. Allen had his first contact with electric railways when Mather and Allen were contracted to handle the engineering of the conversion of Syracuse horsecar lines to electricity and to construct additional new electric railway lines. C. Loomis Allen was put in charge of supervising this portion of the firm's activities. On October 11, 1894, Allen married Miss Florence Rose Worster of Syracuse. They would later have two children, Alfred George and Mary Brown Allen.

Based on his performance with engineering the electric railway tracks of the company, Allen was offered a position with the street railway. On April 15, 1895, Allen left the firm of Mather and Allen and became the civil engineer of the Syracuse Street Railroad Company, the Syracuse Consolidated Street Railway and their successor, the Syracuse Rapid Transit Railway Company. Under Allen's supervision a total of 64 miles of rail lines were either built new or rebuilt and converted to electric operation. Allen first entered electric railway management on March 1, 1898, when he was made assistant general manager of the Syracuse Rapid Transit Railway Company. Allen's performance and a vacancy combined to provide a quick promotion to acting

C. Loomis Allen, from a portrait appearing in *Brill Magazine* in March, 1910. J.R. McFARLANE COLLECTION.

general manager on October 15, 1898, and then to general manager on April 1, 1899.

Allen's success in Syracuse led to job offers at several locations. He decided to make a change with the new year and new century, and on January 1, 1900, he became the general manager of the Lorain Street Railway Company of Lorain, Ohio.

At this time, Horace L. Andrews and John J. Stanley of Cleveland began purchasing and consolidating electric railways in the Syracuse-Utica area. Allen, who was very familiar with this area, effectively became a major part of the local management team for the Andrews-Stanley syndicate. On August 1, 1901, Allen left Lorain and became the engineer and assistant to the general manager of the Utica & Mohawk Valley Railway Company. He subsequently became responsible for other operations as they were acquired by the syndicate.

In 1902, the Andrews-Stanley syndicate acquired control of the Oneida Railway, a 1.5-mile horsecar line. Allen served as president of this company while it was electrified and expanded. 1903 saw the acquisition of the Rome City Street Railway. It was subsequently rebuilt and electrified under Allen as general manager. From 1904 onward, Allen became the general manager of the Andrews-Stanley properties since Andrews and Stanley retained the top slots of president and vice president themselves. However, Allen was effectively the local manager for the syndicate. In June of 1905, he was honored by his old alma mater when Alfred University conferred the honorary degree of Master of Science on Allen.

The situation came full turn for Allen in 1906 when the Syracuse Rapid Transit Railway Company, which he had constructed and managed in the 1890s, was added to the Andrews-Stanley holdings. On December 6, 1906, Allen was elected vice president and general manager of the affiliated companies including the Utica & Mohawk Valley Railway Company, Syracuse Rapid Transit Railway Company, Oneida Railway Company and Rome City Street Railway Company.

Late in 1905, the New York Central & Hudson River Railroad (a predecessor of the huge New York Central system) became a partner of the Andrews-Stanley syndicate in acquiring and expanding electric railway lines. The control of two interurban lines (to Geneva and Sodus Point) was obtained as well as several street and suburban railways in the Rochester area. The control of these lines was vested in the Mohawk Valley Company. In 1907, the Rome City Railway was formally merged into the U&MV. The Oneida Railway was expanded to build and operate a third rail interurban line between Utica and Syracuse over the West Shore Railroad, which was owned by NYC&HR. Allen was, of course, in charge of this electrification project.

A 1908 law of the New York State Public Service Commission prohibited non-railroad holding companies, such as the Mohawk Valley Company, from holding more than 10% of a railroad's common stock. After much paperwork and stock shuffling, the New York State Railways was created on March 22, 1909, to consolidate the Rochester properties and to hold the controlling stock of the affiliated companies. Allen was made a vice president of the New York State Railways and also became third vice president and general manager of the Syracuse, Oneida and Rome-Utica properties. It was during this era, when Allen managed most of the electric railways in the area, that he planned and operated *The Longest Interurban Charter.*

In 1909, Allen became a member of the Board of Trustees of Alfred University. He retained this position for over three decades, until his death.

On January 2, 1912, Allen joined Edward F. Peck of Schenectady, New York in forming the firm of Allen & Peck, Inc. This new company was organized "to promote, reconstruct, reorganize, rehabilitate, engineer and manage public utilities." On March 15, 1912, Allen resigned his positions with the New York State Railways to devote full time to his new firm. On October 15, 1914, he was elected president of the American Electric Railway Association. He also served as president of the New York State Railway Association, the first president of the American Electric Railway Transportation & Traffic Association and became an officer or member of other transportation, civic and fraternal organizations too numerous to mention.

In connection with his work with Allen & Peck, Inc., Allen managed several electric railway companies and was made a railway company officer in the process. The list in 1914 included the presidency of the Newport News and Hampton Railway Gas & Electric Co. of Hampton, Virginia, and the presidency of the Syracuse & Suburban Railroad Company of Syracuse, New York. He was also the vice president of Maryland Electric Railways Co. of Annapolis, Maryland. In October of 1914, Allen & Peck, Inc. was hired to manage the Buffalo, Lockport & Rochester Railway and Allen was made vice president of that company.

On November 1, 1915, Allen returned to the Syracuse area as receiver (with Senator H.S. Holden) of the Beebe syndicate's ill-fated Empire United Railways, Inc. In the summer of 1916, The Rochester, Syracuse & Eastern Railroad was taken out of Empire United Railways and reorganized with Allen as receiver until the new company, Rochester & Syracuse Railroad, was formed on September 19, 1917.

In 1916, both Alfred and Syracuse Universities honored Allen by conferring on him the honory degree of Doctor of Science.

In June of 1918, Allen retired from Allen & Peck, Inc. The firm was then reorganized as Peck-Shannahan-Cherry, Inc. Cherry, Allen's associate and assistant on *The Longest Interurban Charter,* subsequently became involved with managing some of the former Beebe syndicate lines into the 1920s and 1930s.

In 1922, Allen retired from the electric railway industry. He entered the typewriter business and moved to New York City.

In 1932, Allen retired from business and moved to Alfred, New York. Here he devoted himself to the interests of his alma mater, Alfred University. Allen served as a university trustee, chairman of the finance committee, plant manager and head of the student aid committee. He also developed an interest in history and became somewhat of an authority on certain phases of the American Civil War.

Allen passed away at his home in Alfred, New York on September 7, 1941.

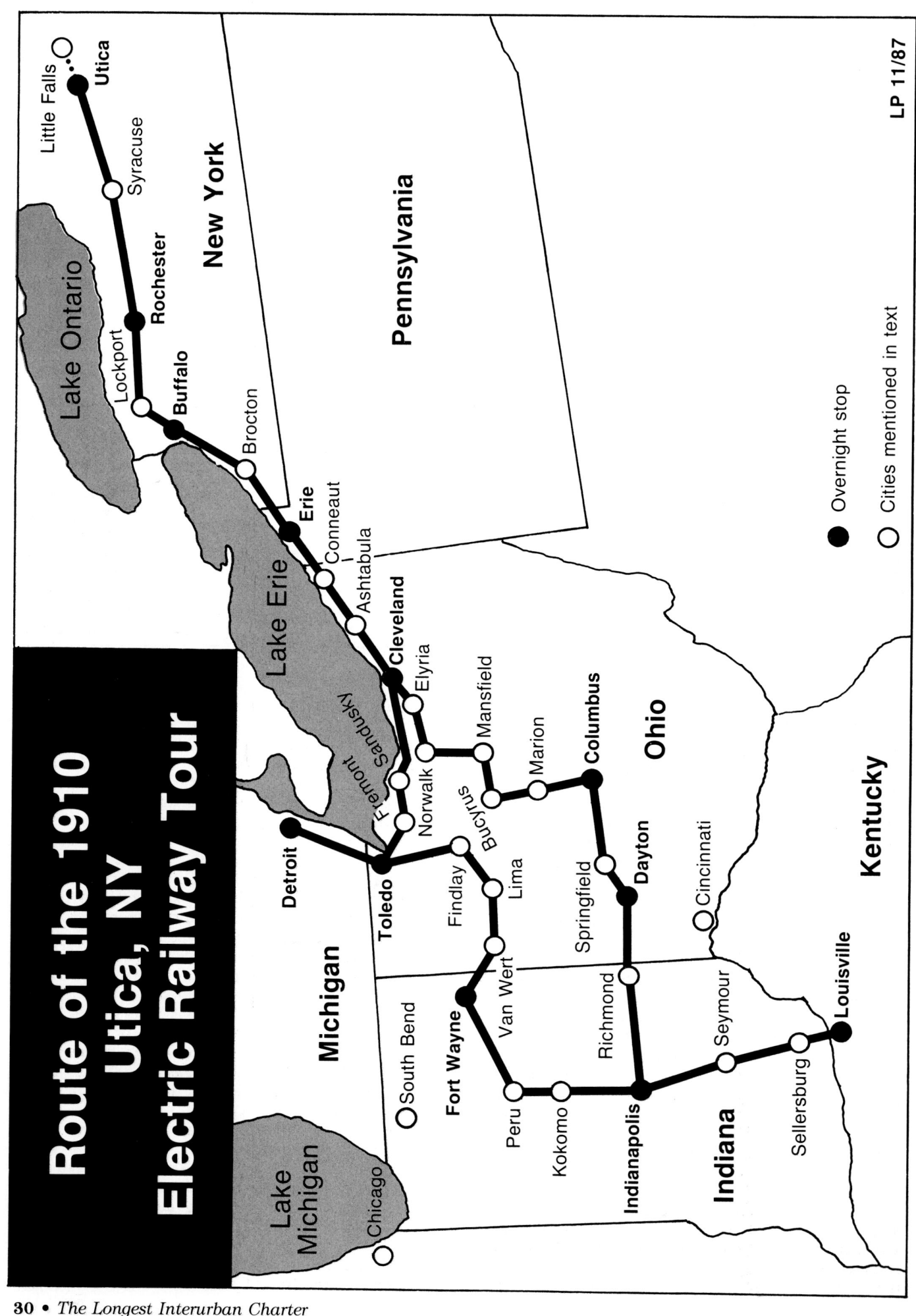

3

The Electric Interurban Odyssey

Tuesday, May 10, 1910
The Grand Start

Car 502 was put on public display at 9:30 a.m. at the Main Street carbarn. Many Utica residents came to inspect the car before its grand departure. With its Pullman green livery and bright gold lettering, car 502 was an impressive sight.

Departure time for the trip had been scheduled for 10:30 a.m. from Bagg's Hotel in downtown Utica, only a block west of the car barn. Passengers in the party had been instructed to arrive at the hotel no later than 10:15 a.m. However, the excitement had started by 10 a.m. when a substantial crowd of Utica residents, newspapermen and local officials had gathered to see the trolley pilgrims off on their trip.

C. Loomis Allen, now designated as transportation chairman for the trip, gathered his passengers in a hotel corridor and announced that all those expected were present. As last-minute preparations and baggage-loading were underway, the crowd gathered around to participate in the final activities before the group's departure.

A large floral horseshoe (of carnations sprinkled thickly with red, pink and yellow roses and trimmed with maidenhair ferns) was given to the trolley pilgrims and presented to Mr. Allen. He placed the horseshoe at the front window of the car. Members of the group were given a watch fob with a small repeating pistol decoration, compliments of the Savage Arms Company. Florist Fred J. Baker, president of the Utica Common Council and a member of the group, gave carnations to each of the men. Tom W. Johnson, a member of the group, and D.M. Johnson gave each of the trolley pilgrims a pocketbook. Other gifts included Utica canes of maple with butternut stain and a quarter bushel of Utica buttons to be distributed on the trip.

Passengers, family and friends were also given a booklet with the itinerary for the trip. For the passengers, it gave them some idea of what was planned for each day. It provided a list of the overnight stops and thus gave families and friends an opportunity to write letters or contact the trolley pilgrims while the trip was underway. It is interesting that the final itinerary distributed on May 10 no longer showed the side trip to Cincinnati.

At 10:25 a.m., car 502 moved to the Main Street entrance of Bagg's Hotel. The car had an American flag draped over its pilot, it sported a destination sign reading "special," and carried white flags indicating it was running as a non-scheduled "extra." The group then boarded the car. Included were General Manager C. Loomis Allen, Superintendent T.C. Cherry, and the other members of the group (other than Arthur Hind, who would be picked up after leaving Utica[1]). Four representatives of the Oneida Railway were on board. They included Superintendent Edward J. Wright, Chief Engineer W.J. Harvie, General Passenger Agent C.R. Gowen and Master Mechanic E.T. Fox. In addition, Charles W. Wicks and D.M. Johnson rode along as far as Rochester. Also on board was the three-man crew consisting of Conductor John O'Hara, Motorman George Moore and Porter William Jackson. It was noted that Jackson wore a handsome white coat while the other members of the crew wore their regular uniforms.

Promptly at 10:30 a.m., Conductor O'Hara sounded two bells and Motorman George Moore solemnly notched up his controller. As the crowd cheered, car 502 pulled away from Bagg's Square and headed up Genesee Street (residents of Utica refer to going south on Genesee Street as "going up"). The street was lined with hundreds of people who waved at the car and the group inside. Miss Carrie R. Sessions (apparently the daughter of Fred W. Sessions, one of the trolley pilgrims) rode horseback by the side of the car until it reached the West Shore Railroad. At the Utica Orphan Asylum, all the children were out on the curb waving flags.

When the car reached the West Shore tracks most of the crowd had been left behind. A brief stop was called in order to photograph the group. For the photograph, the group lined up along car 502 and Allen had the good luck floral wreath placed in the center. The resulting photograph has become the most popular one taken of this trip.

As the car entered the West Shore tracks, which was also the main line of the Oneida Railway, the

This old postcard shows car 502 stopped at the Clark Mills station on a regular eastbound trip from Syracuse to Utica. The photo was probably taken a few months prior to the 1910 Electric Railway Tour. Records indicate that the tour was met by large crowds at this station. ONEIDA COUNTY HISTORICAL SOCIETY.

trolley pole was hooked down and current was collected with the car's under-running third rail shoes. Car 502 then headed west on the first leg of the trip — 49 miles from Utica to Syracuse. A brief stop was made 6 miles west of South Utica at Clark Mills to pick up Arthur Hind.[1] He was the last member of the group to board the car and brought the total passengers to Allen, Cherry and 21 businessmen.

The crowds of people lining the tracks did not end at the city limits of Utica. Large groups were at trackside at Clark Mills, Oneida and Canastota to wave at the trolley pilgrims and wish them luck.

PRECEDING PAGE

The most popular photograph of the 1910 Utica Electric Railway Tour was taken by Utica photographer Albert P. Zintmaster at about 10:45 a.m. on Tuesday, May 10, 1910. The location was the Arnold Avenue crossing of the West Shore tracks where the Oneida Railway cars switched to and from Genesee Street. A 1949 newspaper article lists the participants as follows (from left to right): Motorman George Moore, Conductor John O'Hara, C.Y. Fuller, F.W. Sessions, B. Allen Whiffen, W. Fred Allen, Charles Wicks (directly behind Allen), T.C. Cherry, Tom W. Johnson, J. Soley Cole, Frank J. Baker, Arthur Hind, and William Brock on the left of the horseshoe. At the right of the horseshoe: F.W. Bensberg, Dr. C.T. Guillaume, Wilbur S. Clark, Charles E. Barnard, Jacob Agne, F.A. Cassidy, D.M. Johnson (guest), Charles L. Williams, E.T. Batsford, Henry M. Love, J. Fred McLean, William Schachtel, C. Loomis Allen, John L. Maher and Porter William Jackson. DAVID SCHAFER COLLECTION.

Smaller crowds were noticed in the smaller communities along the Oneida Railway.

The Oneida Railway was not a typical interurban. For most of the distance between Utica and Syracuse, cars operated over the double track line of the steam-powered West Shore Railroad where under-running third rail had been installed. Street operation with a trolley pole was used at both terminal cities and the intermediate community of Oneida. Hence, very little new trackage had been necessary to start interurban service in 1907. Multiple unit cars were used and trains of two or more cars were not unusual. Limited trains averaged over 33 miles per hour between the two terminals. They averaged 42.58 miles per hour between Syracuse and Utica city lines including two positive stops at Oneida and Canastota. This was considerably faster than the average interurban.

At the outskirts of Syracuse, the car left the West Shore tracks with its third rail and entered the tracks of the affiliated Syracuse Rapid Transit Railway. Here, the trolley pole was put up again and the third rail equipment would remain unused until the car returned to Syracuse in two weeks.

Once again the trolley pilgrims were the subject of much attention. Hundreds of Syracuse residents lined the streets between the junction with the West Shore tracks and the downtown interurban station. They caused a flurry of activity in their efforts to get a good look at the Utica car as it passed by.

Car 502 pulled into the Syracuse trolley station at 11:58 a.m. Although manager Allen had known in advance, the trolley pilgrims were surprised to see a Syracuse group awaiting their arrival since there had

The Longest Interurban Charter • 33

Rochester, Syracuse & Eastern car 110 stops for passengers at Port Gibson, New York on a regular run in 1908. Located a few miles east of Rochester, Port Gibson's dusty road and wooden plank passenger platform were not untypical of rural interurban stops at this time. J.R. McFARLANE COLLECTION.

The Rochester, Syracuse & Eastern operated some large and handsome interurban cars between Syracuse and Rochester. Car 110 was built by the Niles Car Co. in 1906. It was 53 feet, 6 inches long, seated 58 passengers and weighed 84,000 pounds. J.R. McFARLANE COLLECTION.

always been a hot rivalry between Syracuse and Utica. The Syracuse Chamber of Commerce was waiting with five automobiles and soon had driven away with most of the trolley pilgrims for a tour of their city. Some of the group went to Syracuse University, others went to Burnet Park, others went to see police headquarters and the remainder went to look at the new Onondaga Hotel which was under construction. The group later rejoined at the Yates Hotel where a luncheon was served courtesy of manager Allen and the Syracuse Chamber of Commerce. Over cigars at the end of the meal, fences were mended between Syracuse and Utica. Mr. Henry M. Love of the trolley pilgrims called for three cheers for manager Allen and the Syracuse Chamber of Commerce for the tour and luncheon. In turn, the Syracuse people called the trolley trip a great idea and wished that they had done it first.

In Syracuse, manager Allen received a telegram from Dr. E.H. Douglas of Little Falls. It read: "Stop, look, listen. Run no blocks. Best wishes."

It is presumed that Superintendent T.C. Cherry and Superintendent Edward J. Wright left the group at Syracuse with the other Oneida Railway officials and returned to Utica. Cherry and Wright were left to run the railroad in Allen's absence although both would later catch up to car 502 and take a turn replacing Allen as transportation manager for the trip.

After returning to car 502, the group was joined by H.C. Beatty, assistant secretary of the Rochester, Syracuse & Eastern Railroad and assistant general manager of the Syracuse, Lake Shore & Northern. Beatty would ride with the group over the 86 miles to Rochester.

At 3 p.m., car 502 left Syracuse and followed SLS&N tracks four miles to Lake Shore Junction. Here, car 502 turned west and entered the tracks of the Rochester, Syracuse & Eastern.

The RS&E was the pride of the Beebe Syndicate and one of the better-constructed interurbans with double track, minimal grades and private right-of-way except through towns. Through interurban service from Rochester to Syracuse started in 1908 via Auburn using the Auburn & Northern and the Auburn & Syracuse. In December of 1909, the RS&E completed its own line to Lake Shore Junction on the outskirts of Syracuse. From this point, RS&E cars operated over the Syracuse Lake Shore & Northern, which had trackage extending into downtown Syracuse except for the city blocks in the Clinton Square Terminal. Hence, the cars did not have to make use of local streetcar tracks to reach the heart of Syracuse.

Mr. H.C. Beatty of the Rochester, Syracuse & Eastern spent a great deal of time explaining features of the new line. The RS&E extended from Syracuse to Rochester and was constructed by the Beebe Syndicate of Syracuse at a cost of $7,000,000.

Power for the car was collected from overhead trolley wire. Between Lake Shore Junction and Weedsport (18 miles), the trolley wire over each track was supported by a single catenary hung from steel towers spaced 300 feet apart. The copper feeders acted as messengers and the trolley wires were held at a uniform 18-foot height above the rail by hangers of varying lengths located every 30 feet along the line. West of Weedsport, standard wood pole and span construction supported a single trolley wire over each track. The initial cost of the steel tower construction was 8% greater than pole type but the cost of maintenance was much less.

Octagonal shelters or waiting rooms were placed at road crossings or stops. They were heated and lighted by electricity and were very convenient and comfortable. The bridge over the Montezuma marshes was 1,500 feet in length, one of the longest trolley bridges in the United States. In portions of this marsh the company put in several hundred thousand yards of earth before getting a good foundation.

The depots were combination passenger and freight stations and were neat and attractive. They were built of open timbered construction with panels filled with pebbled plaster and cost $6,000 each.

As car 502 passed Lyons, the system's power house was pointed out. Steam turbines generated 25,000 k.w. at an average cost of ¾¢ per kilowatt.

The line crossed steam railroads 12 times but not once at grade. All crossings were either overpasses or underpasses.[8] Limited cars could reach a speed of 60 miles per hour.

Entrance to Rochester was made via the local streetcar tracks of New York State Railways. Car 502 arrived in Rochester at 5:50 p.m. in the midst of a light rain. The trolley pilgrims were met and welcomed by officials and members of the Rochester Chamber of Commerce at the Culver Road crossing, the point where RS&E track ownership ended. A dozen automobiles were waiting to take the trolley pilgrims on a tour of Rochester as car 502 was sent on to downtown Rochester over city streetcar tracks. Stops on the automobile tour included various parks, Rochester's new reservoir and other places of interest. It was already dark at 7:30 p.m. when the group went to the Powers Hotel to be entertained at dinner by the Rochester Chamber of Commerce.

Three members of the group were not present for the start of dinner. Two suffered the first mishap of the trip and the third was busy with an important task.

Jacob Agne and another member of the trolley pilgrims were given a tour of Rochester in an automobile by Secretary Woodward of the Rochester Chamber of Commerce and Mr. Osborne, a local nurseryman. Near Charlotte, one of the automobile tires blew out and necessitated a 30-minute delay for the repair. Almost immediately thereafter, a woman stepped in front of the moving auto and was struck a glancing blow. Although she was unhurt, Mr. Osborne insisted on driving the woman home. The two trolley pilgrims then boarded a local trolley car to the Powers Hotel and arrived 30 minutes late for dinner.

The absence of Manager C. Loomis Allen was even more interesting. When the trolley pilgrims and the Rochester Chamber of Commerce sat down to dinner on Tuesday evening, Rochester was still not physically connected to the Midwest interurban network.

When the Buffalo, Lockport & Rochester Railway Company was opened to Rochester in 1908, the tracks stopped short of crossing the Charlotte Branch of the New York Central & Hudson River Railroad on Lyell Avenue on the west side of Rochester at a location known as Otis Station. Passengers to downtown Rochester had to cross the New York Central on foot, walking 80 feet to board a city car of the New York

The Longest Interurban Charter • 35

Between Rochester and Lockport, the trolley pilgrims operated over the tracks of the Buffalo, Lockport & Rochester Railway. Here, in about 1909, we find BL&R car 212 westbound on State Street entering Brockport, New York. Note the unpaved street and the horse and buggy in the distance. J.M. McFARLANE COLLECTION.

The Buffalo & Lake Erie Traction Company operated the interurban line from Buffalo, New York west to Erie, Pennsylvania. It was considered one of the more important and better financed interurbans in the area. Shown is B&LET car 607, a 52-foot combine that was built in 1908 by the Cincinnati Car Company. M.D. McCARTER COLLECTION.

State Railways. The two companies had spent a great deal of time in trying to get permission for a crossing of the New York Central tracks so that BL&R cars could enter Rochester via the streetcar tracks and terminate at the Union Trolley Station in downtown Rochester. The permission was long in coming since it requested a crossing of the two lines at grade — the most dangerous and least desirable type of crossing.

Public Service Commission permission for this crossing had only recently been granted. Some comments recorded this evening suggested that C. Loomis Allen was responsible for getting the crossing in. He reportedly used his influence with the New York Central to accelerate the installation process.

As the trolley pilgrims and the Rochester Chamber of Commerce began assembling for dinner at the Powers Hotel, a track crew began assembling on Lyell Avenue at the New York Central crossing. They were supervised by B.E. Tilton, engineer of maintenance-of-way of the New York State Railways, with the assistance of J.H. Cain, superintendent of the Buffalo, Rochester & Lockport Railway. Manager C. Loomis Allen had brought car 502 to the scene.

Reports indicate that the crew waited for the passage of the 8 p.m. New York Central train and then set to work. A temporary crossing was installed in only 25 minutes. Allen then ran car 502 over the crossing to test it. Plans called for putting in a permanent crossing over the next few days, and for some regular cars to start using the crossing the following Monday.

Meanwhile, dinner at the Powers Hotel was followed by speeches including mention of the railroad crossing. At 11 p.m. the party broke up and the trolley pilgrims retired to the Hotel Seneca for the night.

Although it probably was not known at the time, car 502 and the trolley pilgrims had fostered and been instrumental in an important event in the history of the interurban industry. Less than 100 days earlier, the Winona Railroad had started service between Goshen and Peru, Indiana, thereby completing the missing interurban track link between the northern Indiana/Chicago interurban lines and the other Indiana interurbans which were already connected to lines in Ohio, Pennsylvania and New York. This 80 feet of track in Rochester was the final link of track that would tie in the Midwest interurbans to Little Falls, New York. As such it was the final track link in completing the interurban network.[3]

Frank Dudley, attorney for the Buffalo, Lockport & Rochester Railway later admitted that the crossing was worth at least $65,000 to the interurban line.

Wednesday, May 11, 1910
Rochester to Erie

When boarding car 502 on Wednesday morning, the trolley pilgrims found representatives from the Buffalo, Lockport & Rochester Railway waiting for them. J.M. Campbell, general manager, would ride with the passengers while Superintendent Cain would stay in the cab with Motorman Moore and act as pilot.

Promptly at 9 a.m., car 502 departed from downtown Rochester and headed over streetcar tracks on Main Street and State Street, and then turned west on Lyell Avenue. At Otis Station, General Passenger Agent B.E. Wilson took the controls and guided car 502 over the newly-laid temporary crossing. Once again, car 502 and the trolley pilgrims made history because they were the first passengers to go over the new crossing.

Although planned for double track on a 66-foot wide right-of-way, the Buffalo, Lockport & Rochester never got beyond being a single track line. As such it was the first single-track interurban used by the Utica trolley pilgrims. The line was completed between Rochester and Lockport in November of 1908 and was built to very high standards including minimal grades, a lack of sharp curves and a provision for multiple-unit car operation.

Once past Otis Station and on BL&R tracks, General Manager Campbell began telling the trolley pilgrims about the interurban line.

The road was 58 miles long from Rochester to Lockport and the run was usually made in two hours. Hourly trips were made from 6 a.m. to 11:30 p.m. It was a single track road but stone ballasted all the way so as to make not only smooth but dustless riding.

A change in scenery was noticed by the trolley pilgrims. Monroe, Orleans and Niagara counties were in the fruit-growing belt of western New York. The farms were not all devoted to hay and pasture but ran considerably to fruit trees. There were large vineyards, and large orchards of apples, pears and peaches, many of which were in bloom.

The previous day, H.C. Beatty of the Rochester, Syracuse & Eastern had mentioned that the English pheasant was quite common in the area but none had been spotted recently. Now that Mr. Beatty was no longer on board, the pheasants began bobbing up all around. The interurban men indicated that the pheasants were a hazard after dark since they were apt to fly into the headlight. There was a record of a case where one of the birds broke a front window in the motorman's cab and the broken glass injured the motorman's eyes. Double thick glass was subsequently used in the front window.

About a half-hour after leaving Rochester, Motorman Moore set the car's brakes in Brockport. Moore had spotted a woman in an adjacent yard waving a large flag at the passing car. It was quickly discovered that the woman was Mrs. M.L. Sweeting, a customer of Mr. Fred W. Sessions' millinery business in Utica, who knew when the car was scheduled to pass. This gave Mr. Sessions an opportunity to get off the car briefly to shake hands with his customer and hand out some of the Utica buttons that were being given away on the trip.

Later, a similar brief stop was made in Albion when Ozro Love hailed the car. Mr. Love was 88 years old and the uncle of Henry M. Love, one of the trolley pilgrims on board the car.

At Lockport, car 502 entered the double track of the International Railway Company for the 25-mile run to Buffalo. At this time, BL&R cars would terminate at Lockport and transfer Buffalo passengers to the cars of the IRC. Through BL&R service (using an IRC pilot) was still some years in the future. Car 502 reached Buffalo a few minutes after noon.

Representatives of Buffalo's Chamber of Commerce and Manufacturers' Club, the Wholesale Merchants

The Longest Interurban Charter • **37**

Buffalo & Lake Erie Traction Company car 604 rolls to a stop in Farnham, New York in 1909 while on a westbound run from Buffalo to Westfield. Business must be booming because the car looks crowded, four passengers are waiting to board, and the conductor is handling a suitcase for a passenger getting off. The offending Nickel Plate Railroad bridge that caused much grief to the trolley pilgrims is only a few feet to the front of the car (right in photo). J.R. McFARLANE COLLECTION.

The crew of car 502 are removing the front trolley pole and base in an attempt to squeeze under the Nickel Plate Railroad bridge in Farnham, New York. Several of the trolley pilgrims are standing next to the car and lending moral support. The original photo, reportedly taken by trolley pilgrim John L. Maher, could not be located so this was reproduced from a 1949 copy of the *Utica Observer Dispatch.* ONEDIA COUNTY HISTORICAL SOCIETY.

38 • The Longest Interurban Charter

This photo shows car 502 halfway under the Nickel Plate Bridge at Farnham. John Maher appears to have talked the crew into taking a break while he records the scene for posterity. Reprinted from a 1949 issue of the *Utica Observer Dispatch*. ONEIDA COUNTY HISTORICAL SOCIETY.

Association and both its Extension Committee and Entertainment Committee were waiting for the trolley pilgrims. In addition, J.D.F. Stone and Aikens A. Tallman, both former Uticans, were on hand to provide a welcome. The entire group then went to the Lafayette Hotel at Lafayette Square for a brief luncheon. The representatives from Buffalo expressed regret that the stop in their city was too short to provide a tour. However, they requested the opportunity to provide an elaborate motor car tour on the return trip.

Lafayette Square was also the terminal point for the Buffalo & Lake Erie Traction Company. Upon returning to car 502, the trolley pilgrims were introduced to Julius C. Calish, vice president, and Matthew C. Brush, general manager of the B&LET who would escort them the 93 miles to Erie.

The Buffalo & Lake Erie Traction Company was established late in 1906 as a consolidation of lines operating small segments of the route between Buffalo and Erie. Two predecessor companies (operating local service in Erie and Dunkirk) traced their heritage back to horsecars in 1864. Through service from Buffalo to Erie was not established until late 1909. At this time the company was one of the larger and more prosperous interurban lines in New York state.

At 1:25 p.m., car 502 left Buffalo over the tracks of the Buffalo & Lackawanna Traction Company, a subsidiary of the B&LET, in order to reach the B&LET interurban line to Erie. It was explained that in addition to the Erie interurban and the Lackawanna line, the B&LET operated the Buffalo city line to the Lackawanna steel plant, a branch line to Hamburg and street railway lines in Dunkirk, Fredonia and Erie, a total of 172 miles of electric railways. In addition the same company operated the steam line between Westfield and Jamestown along Lake Chautauqua, as well as boats on Lake Chautauqua.

The trolley pilgrims were told that the Buffalo & Lake Erie Traction Company operated hourly service between Lafayette Square, in the heart of Buffalo, and Erie. In addition, limited trips operated three times a day making only the principal stops.

A strong friendship soon developed between the two interurban officials and the trolley pilgrims. Mr. Calish was a good friend of County Engineer Paul Louis Schultz of Utica. He originally came from Hoboken and was good-naturedly called "Hobokenese." Mr. Brush knew some of the Utica group from a meeting on a previous trip to Washington. Following an invitation, both Calish and Brush agreed to join the group upon their return trip and ride back to Utica.

This turned out to be one of the days when the group ran considerably later than originally planned. The proposed schedule allowed for no significant stops between Buffalo and Erie and called for an arrival time at Erie of 6 p.m. Due to one incident and at least two unplanned stops, the trolley pilgrims were substantially delayed.

One of the more unusual incidents of the trip happened at Farnham at about 2:30 p.m. Then, as now, Farnham is a tiny community 26 miles southwest of Buffalo. Car 502 slowed as it went under the Lake Shore & Michigan Southern Railway bridge and then, a few feet down the road, came to a halt at the Nickel Plate Railroad bridge. Several people got off the car and confirmed their worst fear, that car 502 was too high to go under the bridge. In spite of the fact that the dimensions of car 502 had been sent out well in advance, someone had failed to realize that the car was several inches too tall to fit under this particular bridge.

Disaster was averted when someone pointed out that the adjacent passing track under the bridge was a few inches lower. Hoping for a miracle, the crew backed car 502 down the line and entered the passing track. Upon reaching the Nickel Plate bridge once again, it was discovered that the bridge was still too low to clear the trolley bases. Rather than give up, the crew decided to try removing the trolley bases to see if that would help. The front trolley base was removed and the car narrowly squeezed under the bridge. Then, the same procedure was used with the rear trolley base. Presumably, the crew used a jumper cable to power the car during this procedure. Once clear of the bridge, the trolley bases were re-installed on car 502 and it was able to continue west.

A brief stop was made in Fredonia. The president of the village, Mr. Maytum, and Mr. Otis boarded the car to welcome the trolley pilgrims. They were joined by Mr. Tibbits of Utica who happened to be in Fredonia at this time.

At Brocton, car 502 was put in a siding as the trolley pilgrims went to visit the Brocton Wine Cellars which had been founded by G.E. Ryckman in 1859. The winery had a capacity of up to 500,000 gallons per year. At this time it had 350,000 gallons of wine in storage, which Council President Baker computed was

Cleveland & Erie car 2 was eastbound to Erie when it paused to pick up passengers in downtown East Springfield, Pennsylvania. The diminutive car, unpaved street, and long skirts on the ladies all belong to an era long gone. The photo came from a postcard dated July 4, 1910. DAVID SCHAFER COLLECTION.

Original builder's photo by the Kulhman Car Co. of Cleveland shows Pennsylvania & Ohio car 22 prior to delivery and prior to mounting the trolley poles. The P&O operated this type of car on an hourly headway from Conneaut to Ashtabula and then south to Jefferson. M.D. McCARTER COLLECTION.

more than the number of gallons of water Utica used some years for extinguishing fires. Following a tour, the group was offered a taste of the product and none declined. One account indicates that the trolley pilgrims "reduced this storage by several gallons" and reboarded car 502 "in a fine mood for song." It is presumed that this visit was arranged after leaving Buffalo and was not a part of the original itinerary. Mr. L.R. Ryckman of the wine company boarded car 502 with the group and rode with them as far as Westfield.

The delays this afternoon caused a little bit of consternation in Erie where the trolley pilgrims had originally been scheduled to arrive at 6 p.m. The Erie Chamber of Commerce was all set to welcome the trolley pilgrims and had assembled in their rooms. They waited until 7:30 and since the Uticans had not arrived yet, they went for a quick supper. They were back in their rooms by 8 p.m. and waited another 30 minutes for the Utica group before going into session. Car 502 and the trolley pilgrims finally pulled into Erie at about 8:45 p.m., nearly three hours behind schedule.

Car 502 entered Erie over local streetcar tracks and deposited the group at the entrance to the Reed House Hotel where they were to spend the night. A delegation of Erie businessmen was still waiting to welcome the Uticans. After dinner at the Reed House, some of the trolley pilgrims elected to retire. Others were entertained at the Erie Club. Fred Baker went to the City Hall, had a meeting with the mayor and got all the information he could regarding Erie.

Thursday, May 12, 1910
Erie to Cleveland

Thursday's journey was interesting in that it covered some of the weakest links in the interurban network. The two lines between Erie and Ashtabula served no community larger than Erie and had no major patronage. They were always financially weak, were not substantially constructed and did not offer through passenger cars over connecting lines. The link would only last a dozen years after the passage of car 502.

Thursday morning's departure was at 10 a.m. Car 502 left Erie by going south on Peach Street to 26th Street and then west on 26th Street to the trackage of the Cleveland & Erie Railway. The C&E operated 33 miles of line from downtown Erie, Pennsylvania to Conneaut, Ohio.

The Conneaut & Erie Traction Company began service between the two communities in its corporate name in 1903. Financial difficulties necessitated the reorganization of the company to the Cleveland & Erie Railway in June of 1909. The line never had financial success nor substantial patronage and was known for its lack of reliability and poor service. It used small cars that plodded slowly along single track on side-of-road right-of-way. The C&E was primarily a local carrier and averaged nearly five designated stops per mile of right-of-way. It was probably the weakest line used by the trolley pilgrims and was the first line used to be totally abandoned. It is interesting to note that the C&E was sold at auction to new owners for $200,000 exactly one year prior to the very day that car 502 and the trolley pilgrims passed over the line. Unfortunately, the new management was unable to do anything substantial to improve the condition of the company.

Near Conneaut, car 502 passed over the rebuilt Conneaut River Viaduct which had failed under the weight of a C&E car in 1906. Fortunately, no one was injured at that time because the fast-thinking crew realized what was happening and got their car quickly off the bridge before it fell.

A brief stop was made at Conneaut at the joint interurban depot used by the Cleveland & Erie and the Pennsylvania & Ohio Railway. At Conneaut it was decided to remove the third rail shoes from car 502. While this was going on, a portion of the group went out to inspect the big viaducts that span the valley. Meanwhile, two trolley pilgrims, John L. Maher and F. William Bensberg, wandered into the business section of town. They located a Woolworth store which got their interest because the chain had originated in Utica. Bensberg bought a supply of harmonicas and Maher purchased some flags. Upon their return to car 502 a band (of questionable technique and harmony) was immediately organized.

While making their stop in Conneaut, the trolley pilgrims were advised to set their watches back an hour because they were entering a new time zone.

Service between Conneaut and Ashtabula started in 1901. Like the neighboring Cleveland & Erie, the Pennsylvania & Ohio never enjoyed substantial patronage. Hourly service was provided, but the equipment and trackage were generally of a lesser quality than the typical Midwestern interurban.

Leaving Conneaut, car 502 followed the tracks of the P&O. In spite of its name, the Pennsylvania & Ohio never did reach Pennsylvania. Its interurban line operated 14 miles from Conneaut to Ashtabula and then turned south from Ashtabula for 10 miles to Jefferson. The P&O also operated local lines in both Ashtabula and Conneaut that connected the towns with the nearby shore of Lake Erie.

Car 502 reached Ashtabula at 12:30 p.m. local time. Since this was 1:30 p.m. Utica time, the trolley pilgrims had started to get hungry and discussions had turned to the subject of food. Waiting in Ashtabula to welcome the Uticans were officials of the Cleveland, Painesville & Ashtabula Railroad and the Cleveland, Painesville & Eastern Railroad, two affiliated lines that car 502 would use between Ashtabula and Cleveland. These officials included Joseph Jordan, general manager; E.L. Schmock, secretary and treasurer; and E.C. Flint, division superintendent. When the interurban officials suggested a stop for lunch, the trolley pilgrims quickly agreed.

Consequently, the interurban officials led the way to the Stoll Hotel where a dinner was waiting. The trolley pilgrims were particularly impressed by the Swedish waiters who served the meal.

After dinner, Palmer Wardman, general superintendent and W.B. Atwood, assistant superintendent of the Pennsylvania & Ohio Railway, provided a side trip. A special trolley car was arranged for the group, who boarded and rode three miles north over the local line to Ashtabula Harbor. Here the trolley pilgrims saw the deep harbor where huge iron ore boats were unloaded and the ore transferred to rail cars of the Lake Shore & Michigan Southern Railway. Over 8,000,000 tons of ore were transferred in an 8-month season.

The Longest Interurban Charter • **41**

The Thursday afternoon side trip brought the trolley pilgrims to Ashtabula Harbor. In the distance are the large iron ore boats on Lake Erie while the empty railroad cars to receive the ore are in the foreground. This photo was taken approximately nine years after the visit of the Utica group. DAVE McLELLAN COLLECTION.

A Cleveland, Painesville & Eastern interurban car is shown adjacent to the Willoughby, Ohio station. The CP&E combined with the CP&A to operate hourly service from Cleveland to Ashtabula. M.D. McCARTER COLLECTION.

Although of poor quality, this photograph goes to prove that the Utica Electric Railway Tour was fun as well as business. While in Ashtabula, Ohio the trolley pilgrims encountered a sidewalk straw hat vendor. They could not resist the hats and John Maher could not resist taking a photograph. Modeling the straw hats are Tom W. Johnson and F.W. Bensberg while Charles E. Barnard is on the far left. The car in the background appears to be 502. Reprinted from a 1949 issue of the *Utica Observer Dispatch*. ONEIDA COUNTY HISTORICAL SOCIETY.

On the way back to Ashtabula, the trolley car stopped briefly on a siding near a large school where the children were at recess. Here, the trolley pilgrims distributed more of their Utica buttons while John H. Maher took photos of them.

Mr. Jordan, Mr. Atwood and Mr. Schmock were also on board car 502 when it left Ashtabula. The car travelled over the Cleveland, Painesville & Ashtabula which ran the 27 miles of line between Ashtabula and Painesville. The CP&A was controlled by the Cleveland, Painesville & Eastern which operated 30 miles between Painesville and Cleveland. The combined line operated an hourly headway from Cleveland to Ashtabula. The line between Painesville and Ashtabula had been placed in service in 1903. In 1906, through service between Ashtabula and Cleveland was instituted when the CP&A and the CP&E both came under the same management.

The interurban officers indicated that the line from Painesville to Ashtabula had been in operation for 7 years while the line from Cleveland to Painesville had been in operation for 14 years. Most of the interurban line ran parallel to the shore of Lake Erie at a distance of two to six miles.

A brief stop was made in Painesville for a new pilot. Mr. J.C. Espy, superintendent of transportation for the CP&E, boarded the car. Shortly thereafter, car 502 continued on its way, now officially on the rails of the CP&E. This line between Painesville and Cleveland had originally opened in 1896 and carried a substantial amount of passengers at this time.

An interesting incident took place approaching Mentor. Sharp-eyed Conductor O'Hara recognized a track switch as being of a particular type built by Leary of Utica who worked for James E. Mann on the Bleecker Street road. Superintendent Espy confirmed the fact that it was a Leary switch from Utica and indicated that it was praised by railroad men. In Mentor a few minutes later, the home of ex-president James A. Garfield was pointed out as it was passed.

Shortly after passing Willoughby, the car was flagged down at a place called Rush Road Switch. This was a major junction point on the CP&E since two different routes into Cleveland diverged at this location. Three men boarded the car and began shaking hands and greeting Motorman Moore and Conductor O'Hara as old friends. As the men turned to the trolley pilgrims they were soon identified as former residents of the Utica area who had been instrumental in the development of the Utica & Mohawk Valley interurban line. John J. Stanley was the former general manager, Charles H. Clark was a civil engineer who laid out the road to Little Falls and George L. Radcliffe had been another engineer. All three were currently employed by the Cleveland Electric Railway. Mr. Stanley was their president and general manager, Clark was their chief engineer and Radcliffe was their transportation superintendent. They had decided to take the time to welcome their Utica friends and ride with them to point out the sights on the last few miles of travel into Cleveland.

The Cleveland, Painesville & Eastern had two different routes between Willoughby and Cleveland, both of which were long and slow. The older and shorter route entered Cleveland on trackage of Cleveland's Euclid Avenue streetcar line. The newer Shore Line Route was close to the shore of Lake Erie and entered Cleveland via the St. Clair Avenue streetcar line. At this time the limited cars operated via Euclid Avenue while local cars operated via the Shore Line route.

Car 502 entered Cleveland via Euclid Avenue and the trolley pilgrims were kept busy sightseeing as several

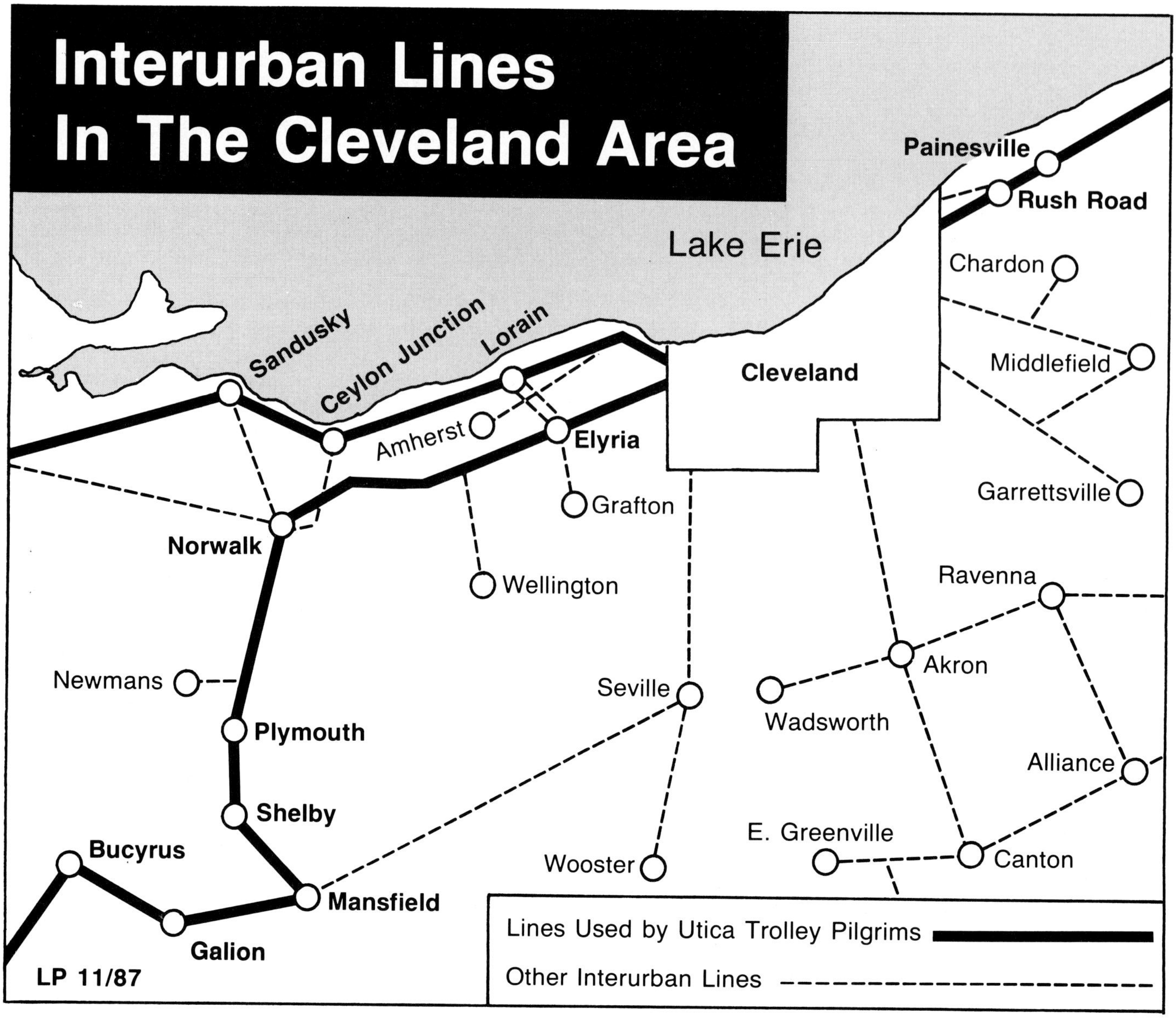

Interurban Lines In The Cleveland Area

Cleveland, Southwestern & Columbus car 122 makes a stop at the Town Hall and interurban station on the public square of Elyria, Ohio. The interurban station, located in the Town Hall behind the car, also housed the dispatcher for the CSW&C western division. The photo was taken in 1906. DAVID SCHAFER COLLECTION.

44 • *The Longest Interurban Charter*

points of interest could be seen from the car. These included the entrance to "Forest Hill" which was the home of John D. Rockefeller, the Stearns Automobile factory, Lake View Cemetery, the Excelsior Club, Western Reserve University and the East End Baptist Church.

The group arrived at the Hollenden House at 8:55 p.m. and were welcomed by several people including some Utica residents. After a late dinner, the trolley pilgrims went out for an evening tour of Cleveland. Later, they returned to the Hollenden House where they spent the night.

One of the trolley pilgrims wrote that car 502 had been carefully "stabled" each night and cleaned before the morning's departure. The electric railway people along the way were impressed with the car and frequently asked technical questions. The Uticans were not able to answer the questions and referred them to Conductor O'Hara and Motorman Moore who usually provided the desired information.

The three-man crew, consisting of O'Hara, Moore and Jackson, did most of the cleaning and some of the inspection work on car 502. Each night they would take the car to the designated trolley barn or yard. Then they would put on overalls and set to work. First, they went under the car to check the motors and running gear. After this they cleaned the inside and outside of the car and polished the windows and woodwork. On many occasions the trolley pilgrims would be sleeping before the crew got back from the car barn to eat their supper. But each morning the car was sparkling clean and very presentable. It attracted considerable attention of the locals while standing in the street at the hotel waiting for its travellers. Some of the interurban lines had cars 10 feet longer than the 502 but it was felt that nowhere was there a more attractive or comfortable car.

Friday, May 13, 1910
Cleveland to Columbus

Fortunately, none of the trolley pilgrims were overly superstitious. If they were, the omen of Friday the thirteenth might have been too much to bear. As it was, the day turned out to be one of the longest and most difficult of their entire trip. The trolley pilgrims lost the able leadership of the individual who had planned and guided the trip from the start. And, on the same day, they were scheduled to travel the longest distance covered on any day of the trip with intermediate stops. Due to the distance to be run and the lack of time, no stop would be made for lunch. This was the only day of the trip when the trolley pilgrims would eat a meal on board the car.

Manager C. Loomis Allen left the group with a promise to rejoin them in a few days. No reason was given for Allen's absence. However, it is surmised that he used a few days in the Midwest to conduct company business, possibly including visiting interurban car builders. Within two years the Oneida Railway would take delivery of two new steel cars from the G.C. Kuhlman Car Company of Cleveland. T.C. Cherry joined the group in Cleveland. Cherry had ridden on car 502 on the first leg of its journey from Utica to Syracuse but had remained in the Utica area for a few days to attend to business matters. In Allen's absence, Cherry acted as transportation manager for car 502 and the trolley pilgrims.

Arrival at Cleveland marked a substantial change for the trolley pilgrims. Until they reached Willoughby, on the outskirts of Cleveland, there was only one practical route for car 502 to follow. However, Cleveland was a major center of interurban operation. A total of five companies operated a total of nine different interurban lines radiating from Cleveland, three of which connected with the Midwest interurban network. Hence, for the first time, the trolley pilgrims were in an area that offered multiple connections and multiple routing possibilities.

Before leaving Cleveland on Friday morning, the group gathered in front of the Hollenden Hotel for a photograph. Four individuals joined the trolley pilgrims this morning. Three were officials of the Cleveland, Southwestern & Columbus Railway, Vice President A.E. Akins, Superintendent and General Manager E.F. Scheider and western division Superintendent J.A. Nester. The fourth individual was G.E. Faber of Wapakoneta, Ohio. Faber had relatives in Utica and was a frequent visitor there.

Car 502 left Cleveland at 9 a.m. and headed west on Lorain Avenue streetcar tracks for about five miles to reach the Cleveland, Southwestern & Columbus Railway tracks. The group then headed west to Norwalk approximately 58 miles from Cleveland. The last extension into Norwalk had been put in operation in 1902 although the line from Cleveland to Elyria dated from 1895.

At Elyria, the car was hailed by Mrs. Cherry and her mother, Mrs. John Lersch. The two ladies were invited to get on board and ride as far as they wished. They were welcomed by the trolley pilgrims who were happy to have a pleasant change from all-male company.

What remains a mystery is why car 502 was routed to Columbus via Norwalk and Shelby rather than via Seville. The Cleveland, Southwestern & Columbus was the largest independent interurban in the state of Ohio. The only larger operation was the Ohio Electric Railway which consolidated or leased several other lines. Throughout its lifetime, the Cleveland, Southwestern & Columbus had two main routes from Cleveland. Newer of the routes, and the shorter to Columbus, was south from Cleveland to Seville and then west to Mansfield (completed in 1908), and on to Bucyrus. However, car 502 took the longer route west from Cleveland to Norwalk. From Norwalk south to Mansfield it was necessary to use the tracks of other interurban lines. On occasion, one-day circle tours had been operated by the Cleveland, Southwestern & Columbus. They reached Mansfield via one route and returned by the other, using the two intermediate interurban lines between Norwalk and Mansfield. Other than the stop in Elyria to pick up Mrs. Cherry and her mother, no record survives of another stop between Cleveland and Mansfield that would have dictated use of the longer route via Norwalk.

Once underway, the officials of the Cleveland, Southwestern & Columbus lost little time in telling the trolley pilgrims about their line and its history.

The company operated 215 miles of track and most of the system was supplied from a power house at

Birmingham, Ohio is located approximately midway between Elyria and Norwalk. On the Cleveland, Southwestern & Columbus this stop merited a substantial brick building that served as both an electric substation and a passenger station. Here, CSW&C car 123 stops adjacent to the awning of the Birmingham station on an eastbound run to Cleveland. DAVID SCHAFER COLLECTION.

This pre-1910 photo shows a three-car meet at Newman's Corners on the Sandusky, Norwalk & Mansfield Electric Railway. From left to right you have the shuttle car heading around the curve to Chicago Junction, the southbound car to Shelby and the northbound car to Norwalk. Chicago Junction (now known as Willard) was a Baltimore & Ohio Railroad station at the intersection of its east-west and north-south lines that provided interurban passengers with connections to several cities. DAVID SCHAFER COLLECTION.

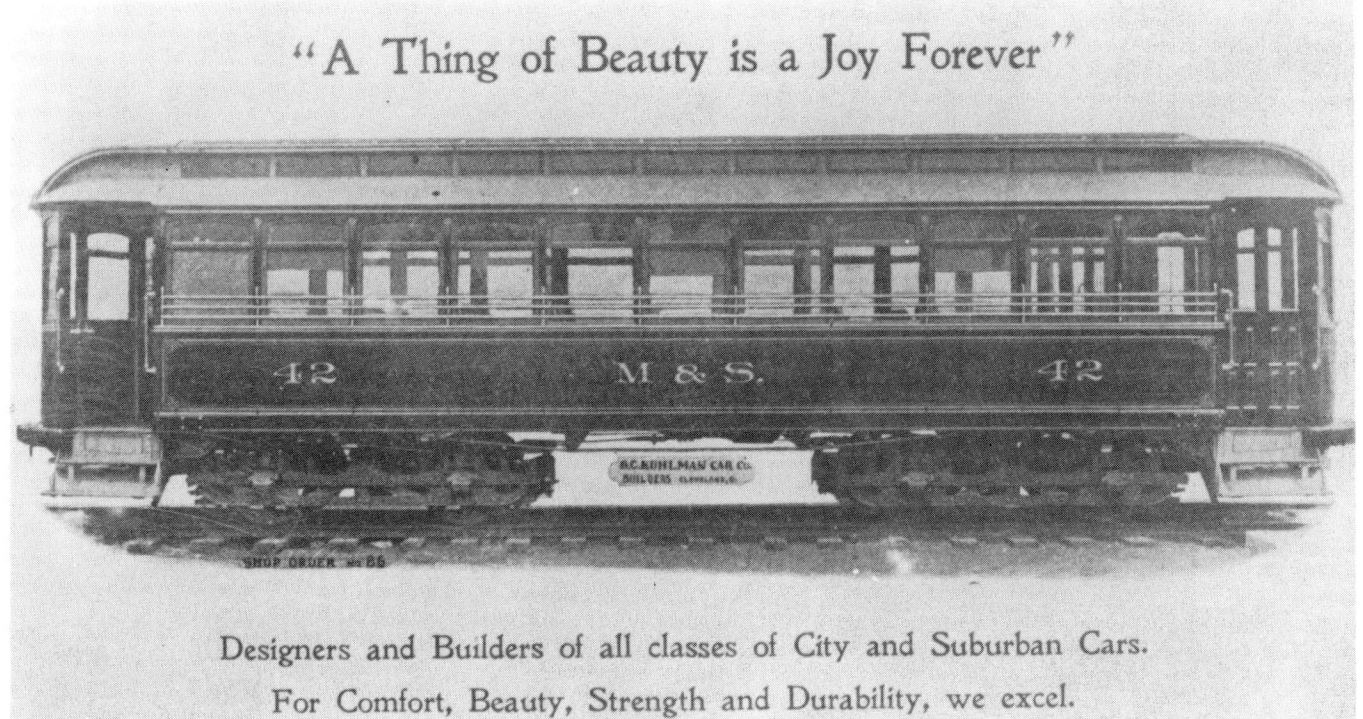

This builder's photo from the Kuhlman Car Company shows Mansfield & Shelby car 42 after construction but prior to delivery. The trolley poles had not yet been affixed to the car at the time of this photo. DAVID SCHAFER COLLECTION.

Elyria which had three large steam turbines. In addition to passengers, the company carried package freight and as many as 1,200 to 1,500 cans of milk daily.

The company was founded in Berea as a one-mile horsecar line connecting the village with a railroad station. An extension was made into Cleveland and the first cars were equipped with storage batteries until trolley wires were put up. Since then the company had had a rapid growth. There were no heavy grades on the line which made high speed operation possible.

Surviving records indicate that car 502 covered the first 58 miles from Cleveland in only 1½ hours. This was excellent time and is difficult to believe since it would have been nearly an hour faster than scheduled cars on this division. However, when the Southwestern was first built there were frequent rate and time "wars" with the competing Lake Shore Electric between Norwalk and Cleveland. Southwestern's best time was 1 hour and 30 minutes while Lake Shore Electric's best was 1 hour and 20 minutes, both set in a race that took place on December 11, 1903.

At Norwalk, car 502 switched to the rails of the Sandusky, Norwalk & Mansfield Electric Railway. This line was followed south to Shelby, a distance of 25 miles. The trackage between Plymouth and Shelby had been completed in 1907. With little patronage, the SN&M was one of the weakest lines in Ohio and discontinued electric operations in 1921.

In Shelby, S.A. Foltz, general manager of the Mansfield Railway Light and Power Company boarded car 502. He guided the car south over his line to Mansfield, a distance of 12 miles. This line had been in operation since 1901 and was the shortest interurban line used by the Uticans.

Mansfield marked the first real stop of the day. Here the group left the car to line up in front of the Soldier's Monument. Relatives of the Utica residents welcomed the group and were promptly given some of the Utica buttons brought along.

Mr. E. Johnson, superintendent of the southern division of the Cleveland, Southwestern & Columbus boarded the car in Mansfield. He would guide the car the 29 miles west to Bucyrus.

Less than an hour after leaving Mansfield, car 502 was held up at Galion by a group of boosters from Bucyrus who had come out 12 miles to board the car. Included were F.L. Hopley, secretary of the Bucyrus Industrial Association, Probate Judge Charles Schavor and several others. By way of credentials, the group carried a letter from George Whysall, president of the Central Electric Railway Association.[4] The letter read in part: "The small towns in this territory as well as some of the larger ones feel hurt by reason of your inability to spend a day in each one viewing the unsurpassed advantages obtainable for any line of business. You will do well to keep close tabs on this crowd, otherwise they will be attempting to move Utica industries to their town."

While traveling the last 12 miles to Bucyrus, the Utica group was informed on business and industry in Bucyrus and the fact that five new industries had come to the community during the past year. The Bucyrus group also mentioned Walter Crittenden, a former Utican, who was connected with the manufacture of steam shovels and dredges.

Upon its arrival in Bucyrus, car 502 was subject to a substantial change in passengers as people left the car and others boarded.

The Cleveland, Southwestern and Columbus Railway people left car 502 at Bucyrus because it was the end of their track. George Whysall, president of the Columbus, Marion & Bucyrus Railroad, boarded car 502 at this point. The CM&B operated 18 miles of track between Bucyrus and Marion. It was affiliated with the

This photo from a 1910-era postcard shows East Main Street in Galion, Ohio. Based on the number of people waiting on the street we can assume that eastbound and westbound cars of the Cleveland, Southwestern & Columbus are meeting at the interurban depot. DAVID SCHAFER COLLECTION.

Many interurban and trolley lines used company-owned parks as a means of generating additional ridership and revenue. This pre-1908 photo shows a car of a predecessor to the Cleveland, Southwestern & Columbus unloading passengers at the entrance to Seccaium Park, about six miles east of Bucyrus. Car 502 and the trolley pilgrims would pass by this same point in 1910. DAVID SCHAFER COLLECTION.

Columbus, Delaware & Marion car 40 was photographed while turning a corner on an unidentified city street. Note following car in the distance. M.D. McCARTER COLLECTION.

Columbus, Delaware & Marion Railway which operated between the cities of its corporate name. The Columbus, Marion & Bucyrus was a smaller and lightly-patronized interurban line that existed primarily as a link between the two larger lines to Columbus and Cleveland. Normal service was provided by a single car that shuttled back and forth on the line providing a two-hour headway. Service between Bucyrus and Marion had started in 1908.

The Bucyrus group also left the car but they were immediately replaced by a similar group from Marion that had travelled to Bucyrus to meet the Uticans. Included were bank president J.E. Waddell, Earl T. Smart, president of the Marion Merchants Association, and several others. The Marion group was led by former Ohio Lieutenant Governor Warren G. Harding.[5]

While car 502 left Bucyrus and headed south to Marion, the Marion group discussed their fair city with the trolley pilgrims. Harding and his friends insisted on taking the Uticans for a tour of the large Marion Steam Shovel Works. Harding spent much of his time in conversation with newspaperman William Schachtel and Secretary J. Soley Cole. Cole later reported that Harding's manner was "as easy as an old shoe."

After arriving in Marion at 3:50 p.m., the trolley pilgrims were given a tour of about a dozen of the 70 buildings making up the Marion Steam Shovel Works. Mr. Busby P. Sweeney, superintendent of the shops of the steam shovel works, conducted the tour. The group was also given the opportunity to inspect a machine reported to be the largest steam shovel in the world.

When car 502 left Marion at 4:30 p.m. it was virtually devoid of guests for the first time in hours. The only individual boarding at Marion was J.R. Harrigan, the general manager of the Columbus, Delaware & Marion Railway. He would guide the car for the 50 miles from Marion to Columbus, the last leg of Friday's travels. This line had opened in 1903 and was built to relatively high standards.

At the time of the passage of the trolley pilgrims, both the Columbus, Delaware & Marion and the affiliated Columbus, Marion & Bucyrus were in bankruptcy due to the expense of building the 18-mile link between Marion and Bucyrus.

At Delaware, a brief stop was made to pick up some newspaper men. Representatives from both Delaware and the *Columbus News* boarded the car and rode with the trolley pilgrims. The Utica trip was apparently big news in Columbus and the reporters were out to get their stories and interview the passengers.

Car 502 pulled into Columbus at 6:16 p.m. and the Uticans immediately went to the Chittenden Hotel. Here they were greeted by a Columbus group who offered to take them on an evening tour of the city. Although tired from their long trip, the trolley pilgrims agreed to the sightseeing.

The Uticans were particularly impressed by a wide bridge near the railroad station that carried a main Columbus street across 20 tracks of the Pennsylvania Railroad. Two streetcar lines also used this crossing, which had a clearance of 24 feet above the railroad tracks. Other stops included the State Capitol Building and a demonstration of the big flushing tanks used to clean the pavements. After the sightseeing, the trolley pilgrims gratefully returned to the Chittenden Hotel to retire for the night.

Saturday, May 14, 1910
Columbus to Dayton

The trolley pilgrims were undoubtedly unhappy about getting up at 5:30 a.m. because of an early departure. Tom W. Johnson was responsible for getting the group started each morning. He made an early check to see that everyone was up and their suitcase ready for departure. He then arranged to have the baggage transferred to car 502 and settled accounts with the hotel.

F.T. Moore, superintendent of the Ohio Electric Railway, boarded car 502 prior to its 7 a.m. departure. Today's brief travel would cover 75 miles of Indianapolis, Columbus & Eastern track from Columbus to Dayton through Springfield.

Interurban service between Columbus and Springfield started in 1901. Service between Springfield and Dayton had been in operation since

Ohio Electric Railway car 68 heads a three-car train on a special charter movement. Car 68 was a 61-foot combine built by the Cincinnati Car Co. in 1912. M.D. McCARTER COLLECTION.

John Maher took this photo of the interior of car 502 while the Utica Electric Railway Tour was underway. Identifiable men in the photo (left to right) include: Tom W. Johnson, W. Fred Allen, F.A. Cassidy, Charles L. Williams, Frank J. Baker, E.T. Batsford, Dr. T.C. Guillaume and William Schachtel. The photo was reproduced from a 1949 issue of the *Utica Observer Dispatch*. ONEIDA COUNTY HISTORICAL SOCIETY.

Most of the interurban lines used by the trolley pilgrims were single track lines which necessitated taking siding at intervals to pass a car or train going in the opposite direction. The trolley pilgrims got into the habit of pitching pennies next to car 502 while waiting on a siding. The camera of John Maher caught F.W. Bensberg showing his penny-pitching technique. Shown in the photo, from left to right, are Tom W. Johnson, F.A. Cassidy, Charles E. Barnard, W. Fred Allen, Bensberg, Wilbur S. Clark and Jacob Agne. The photo was reproduced from a 1949 issue of the *Utica Observer Dispatch.* ONEIDA COUNTY HISTORICAL SOCIETY.

1900. In 1906, these lines were leased by the Indianapolis, Columbus & Eastern Traction Company. The Ohio Electric then leased the IC&E in 1907.

It is easy to imagine the interior of car 502 with one line of wicker chairs along each side in a formal row. However, that was not the situation at all and daytime travel for the trolley pilgrims was considerably less formal. Many of the wicker chairs were scattered randomly around the car's interior as small groups got together for conversation and others sought a quiet corner to read a newspaper. Some remained by the windows and spent much of their time watching the passing scenery. Two card tables were often in use and the players were usually ringed by a group of kibitzers.

C. Loomis Allen participated in very few of the social activities on board the car. He was always in the front seat of the forward compartment so he could see what was ahead and supervise operations.

Operating as an "extra," car 502 frequently had to duck into a siding to allow a regularly scheduled interurban car to pass going in the other direction. Some of the trolley pilgrims got into the habit of pitching pennies beside the car while awaiting the arrival of the other car in the "meet." Fred W. Bensberg reportedly had the best penny-pitching technique.

Car 502 arrived at Third and Jefferson Streets in downtown Dayton at 9:50 a.m. and the trolley pilgrims were welcomed by a delegation including local businessmen, members of the Dayton Chamber of Commerce and representatives of the National Cash Register Company.[6] The Uticans were soon taken to the National Cash Register plant since it closed at noon on Saturday and it was best to see the plant when in operation. The trolley pilgrims went in car 502 while the Dayton group used chartered streetcars.[7]

After the tour of the NCR plant, the trolley pilgrims were given a lecture on NCR operations and were surprised by being shown photos of themselves and of buildings in Utica. It was later discovered that the photos had been obtained by the National Cash Register agent in Utica and by Mr. Sessions' daughter. This was followed by a substantial lunch at the National Cash Register Officer's Club.

Early afternoon found the trolley pilgrims riding car 502 back to downtown Dayton. They got off at the Algonquin Hotel where they would spend the night. The Uticans spent the afternoon sightseeing, including a visit to the National Soldier's Home which housed 4,000 veterans. From there they went to the factory district of Dayton and a residential area.

The initial itinerary of the Utica Electric Railway Tour contemplated a side trip to Cincinnati. The plan anticipated a departure from Dayton late Saturday afternoon and then running the 54 miles to Cincinnati via the Ohio Electric Railway. Saturday night would have been spent in Cincinnati and they would have looked around the city on the following morning. They would have returned to Dayton on Sunday afternoon and then immediately headed west. This portion of the trip was cancelled "because of unexpected obstacles" and the group instead enjoyed a leisurely stay in Dayton. Surviving records indicate that this change of plans took place prior to the group's departure on May 10. However, one of the Dayton newspapers actually reported the group as having departed for Cincinnati.[8]

After discharging their group at the Algonquin Hotel, Motorman Moore, Conductor O'Hara, and Porter William Jackson took car 502 to be serviced. This involved a trip of 12 miles to a large car barn. As they passed through Fairfield, the trio noticed hundreds of

The trolley pilgrims pose in front of car 502 after arriving in Dayton. The photo was reproduced from a 1910 Dayton newspaper. ONEIDA COUNTY HISTORICAL SOCIETY.

Below: Car 78 crosses the Indiana-Ohio State Line on the old Dayton & Western line in 1910. The automobile on the adjacent road was an example of what would happen to interurban passengers in the years to come. DAVID SCHAFER COLLECTION.

Terre Haute, Indianapolis & Eastern Traction Company interurban car 43 passes line car 105 on a siding on typical country right-of-way. Car 43 was a 61-foot combine built by the Cincinnati Car Company in 1912. The block signal (left) dates this photo as being several years after the passage of the trolley pilgrims. M.D. McCARTER COLLECTION.

automobiles, horse teams and many people along the highway. The cause was apparent when one of the Wright airships rose from the ground and began "circulating." They later found out that the Wrights were working on a contract for five flying machines for a fair in Indianapolis at a price of $50,000.

The Wright airship became a topic of discussion among the Uticans because none of them other than the crew had ever seen an airship off the ground.

Sunday, May 15, 1910
Dayton to Indianapolis

Time was allowed on Sunday morning for church services. Early afternoon was spent on continued sightseeing in Dayton with emphasis on parks and public buildings. Dayton was crowded on Sunday with a convention of the Woodmen of the World. The trolley pilgrims were impressed by their neat uniforms which included an axe hung from their left hip by a belt.

The trolley pilgrims left Dayton at 3 p.m. going west on the Dayton & Western Traction Company that operated 40 miles to Richmond, Indiana. It is presumed that F.T. Moore of the Ohio Electric Railway was still on board as a pilot since reports indicate he had been assigned to the group while on Ohio Electric trackage.

The Dayton & Western began service between Dayton and Richmond in 1903. In that same year, a through link between Richmond and Indianapolis had been completed. This eventually became the most important of the three links between the Ohio and Indiana interurbans. In 1907, the Ohio Electric obtained a lease of the line.

Over the state line in Richmond, car 502 entered the tracks of the Terre Haute, Indianapolis & Eastern Traction Co. This line was used for 69 miles from Richmond to Indianapolis. The Terre Haute, Indianapolis & Eastern Traction Company was formed in 1907 from several predecessor companies although the line from Richmond to Indianapolis had been in operation since 1903. This line was single track but generally operated substantial equipment on frequent schedules. The THI&E operated several lines out of Indianapolis and was generally considered the second largest interurban in Indiana.

By this time the Uticans had spent five nights away together and numerous hours on car 502 in each others' company. Letters to friends and relatives back home mentioned interesting or unusual incidents.

Several of the trolley pilgrims were impressed by the activities of the many Chambers of Commerce in the cities visited. Four members of the trolley pilgrims, who were not members of the Utica Chamber of Commerce asked for application blanks.

Charles Barnard got a reputation as the noisiest individual in the group. He invented a "war whoop" that immediately drew everyone's attention.

Fred Cassidy lost his hat in a high wind but Fred Sessions helped him pick out another. The new hat was described as a "very fetching near-Parisian creation, sort of a cross between a Gainesboro and a Toque." Fred began wearing a brilliant hat pin to keep his new hat from blowing away.

The Longest Interurban Charter • **53**

Main Street, Edinburg, Indiana shortly after 1910, as shown on a postcard mailed in 1915. A northbound Indianapolis, Columbus & Southern combine approaches the Edenburg Station in the late afternoon of a summer day. Some of the IC&S officials joined the trolley pilgrims at this point. JERRY MARLETTE COLLECTION.

Indianapolis & Louisville car 202 rolls south through Austin, Indiana on a November, 1907 afternoon. The I&L was the only line used by the trolley pilgrims where car 502 could not operate under its own power. Because of the 1,200-volt direct current, car 502 had to be towed over this line. DR. CARL BOGARDUS SR./JERRY MARLETTE COLLECTION.

Car 502 and the Uticans arrived in Indianapolis at 7 p.m. The group went to the Hotel Claypool, where they spent the night. There was a reception committee waiting but no activities were recorded for Sunday evening. Sightseeing in Indianapolis was planned for the following Tuesday and Wednesday when the group would return to Indianapolis.

Monday, May 16, 1910
Indianapolis to Louisville

Monday morning saw the Utica group embark on the leg of their journey which would take them the farthest distance from home. Three interurban lines had created an electric railway link between Indianapolis and Louisville. The final segments (Columbus-Seymour and Seymour-Sellersburg) had been completed and put in operation in 1907. Through service between Indianapolis and Louisville had started in 1908.

Car 502 left Indianapolis at 8 a.m. on Indianapolis Railway streetcar tracks on Virginia and Shelby Avenues and then entered the interurban trackage of the Indianapolis, Columbus & Southern Traction Company, which was followed to Seymour, a distance of 62 miles.

At Edinburg, about 32 miles outside of Indianapolis, a stop was made for officials of the IC&S. Boarding car 502 was 86 year-old Joseph I. Irwin, the company president. He was accompanied by Vice President William G. Irwin and Z.T. Sweeny, Irwin's brother-in-law. The Irwin family owned the IC&S and lived in Columbus. This group remained on board for only a few miles.

Car 502 was flagged down at one of the smaller way stations. Passengers and crew anticipated some new train orders or a notice of some problem ahead. Instead, they were pleasantly surprised when they were handed a telegram from the Louisville Board of Trade inviting them to be their guests at Churchill Downs. The answer was an expected "yes."

At Seymour, the Utica group ran into their only power compatibility problem of their entire trip. The tracks between Seymour and Sellersburg were built by the Indianapolis & Louisville Traction Company and the overhead wire was electrified with a somewhat uncommon 1,200-volt direct current system. As a consequence, the I&L cars operated all through service from Indianapolis to Louisville since they could also operate on the conventional 600-volt direct current systems of the adjoining two interurban lines by throwing a switch in the car.

Since arriving in Syracuse several days previously, Oneida Railway car 502 had successfully been able to operate on its own on the connecting interurbans by using a trolley pole and 600-volt direct current. However, it could not operate on the higher I&L voltage.

Boarding the car at Seymour was H.D. Murdock, general superintendent of the Indianapolis & Louisville Traction Company, who formerly resided in Cooperstown, New York. The Utica group had a brief wait until an Indianapolis & Louisville car was coupled to the front of their car. Car 502 was then towed the 41 miles to Sellersburg under the high voltage trolley wires.

Motorman George Moore was very complimentary of the trackage between Indianapolis and Louisville. He indicated that the first 62 miles to Seymour were well ballasted with gravel. The remaining 55 miles from Seymour to Lousiville had a stone ballast.

A slight delay was encountered at Scottsburg when it was discovered that some of the third rail equipment on car 502 projected too far from the side of the car to clear a platform. A portion of the offending platform was quickly removed and the train with the I&L car pulling car 502 continued south.

At Sellersburg, a stop was made to detach the I&L car and allow the Utica car to put up its trolley pole and take power once again from conventional 600-volt overhead. F.E. Cole, superintendent of the Louisville & Northern Railway boarded car 502 and escorted the trolley pilgrims the remaining 14 miles to Louisville.[9]

In Jeffersonville, the car went up the ramp to the Big Four Railroad bridge and crossed the Ohio River. The Louisville streetcar system was built to the unusual gauge of five feet and could not be used. However, the interurban line had constructed standard gauge track to connect the Big Four Railroad bridge to Louisville's Interurban Depot.

Louisville was effectively the end of the interurban network in this part of the country. The Louisville & Interurban Railroad operated some short routes out of Louisville, but none provided further connections and all but the Prospect line were built to the five-foot gauge of the Louisville streetcar system.

Car 502 arrived in Louisville at 1:40 p.m. and pulled into the "station of the Big Red Cars" on Third Avenue between Green and Walnut Streets. The Uticans were welcomed by Mayor W.O. Head, a reception committee and members of the Louisville Board of Trade. The group then retired to the nearby Board of Trade Building for a formal welcome. After this, the visitors were served a bountiful buffet in the Director's Room.

Mayor Head indicated that the trolley pilgrims could be their guests at Churchill Downs that afternoon. The mayor said that the Governor of New York made it a crime to bet on a horse race but in Kentucky, horse racing was the sport of kings and every individual had the privilege to back a horse without violating the law. Mayor Head was quoted as saying: "Some of you may bet with ill luck but should any of you go broke, gentlemen, our pocketbooks are at your disposal." Attorney Henry M. Love of Utica responded by suggesting that Utica should be annexed to Louisville.

Following lunch, the group left the Board of Trade Building and boarded chartered streetcars that were waiting at the door. The Louisville streetcars carried everyone to Churchill Downs for a look at the race track and grounds. The trolley pilgrims were impressed by the spacious Club House and stayed for six races. They learned that the Kentucky Derby had had its 36th running earlier in the month and was won by a horse named Donau.

Ten of the trolley pilgrims decided to put $10 each into a betting pool and try their luck with the horses. The result of the first few races was nearly a disaster as they won nothing and only $30 remained in the pool. Taking pity on the Uticans, Mayor Head suggested a "sleeper" in the last race that was going to the post

Interurbans from the north entered Louisville on the Big Four Bridge over the Ohio River. This scene, dating from about 1917, looks north from the Louisville side of the river and shows an interurban crossing the bridge. CAUFIELD & SHOOK COLLECTION, UNIVERSITY OF LOUISVILLE PHOTOGRAPHIC ARCHIVES.

with 20-to-1 odds. He indicated that his own money would be on that horse. Tom Johnson decided to follow the mayor's advice and put the last $30 on the suggested horse. The horse came in and the group decided to use the winnings to throw a party for the trolley pilgrims and their Louisville friends.

After the races, the group again boarded their chartered streetcars and returned to downtown Louisville. Here they checked into the new Seelbach Hotel where they were to spend the night. The winnings from Churchill Downs were soon applied towards a dinner and the Louisville representatives were invited to stay. Many members of Louisville's reception committee remained for dinner, which was followed by speeches and discussion. Clarence Dallam, attorney for the Louisville Traction Company, placed a streetcar at the disposal of the Utica group for any trip they would like to take on Tuesday. The group finally broke up at 10:30 p.m.

Tuesday, May 17, 1910
Louisville to Indianapolis

On Tuesday morning the trolley pilgrims took advantage of the traction company's offer and used a private streetcar to tour Louisville. Their first stop was the city water works and filter plant. The plant itself cost $2,000,000 and kept the Uticans' attention for several hours. From here the group went to City Hall to pay a brief visit to Mayor Head.

Next, the Uticans boarded their private Louisville streetcar once again and rode to the Rugby Distillery. Here they watched straight whiskey being made. After watching every process in the plant, they were entertained at a luncheon.

The Uticans elected to return to downtown Louisville via some sightseeing in the tobacco warehouse district. This took more time than anticipated and they were nearly late for their departure.

PRECEDING PAGE

A 1913 view of city streetcars in Louisville looking north on 4th Street from a point just south of Walnut. This location is only one block over from the interurban terminal and would have been the steetcar route of the trolley pilgrims to Churchill Downs. UNIVERSITY OF LOUISVILLE PHOTOGRAPHIC ARCHIVES.

The Longest Interurban Charter • **57**

Louisville's Third Street interurban terminal soon after it was enlarged in 1908. This was the arrival and departure point for the trolley pilgrims in Louisville. CAUFIELD & SHOOK COLLECTION, UNIVERSITY OF LOUISVILLE PHOTOGRAPHIC ARCHIVES.

Car 401 of Interstate Public Service (successor to the three lines between Indianapolis and Louisville) passes a city car on Spruce Street in downtown New Albany, Indiana. The car will soon cross the Big Four Bridge and will terminate at the Third Street terminal in Louisville. UNIVERSITY OF LOUISVILLE PHOTOGRAPHIC ARCHIVES.

While in Indianapolis, the trolley pilgrims undoubtedly took a few minutes to explore the Indianapolis Traction Terminal. The entire complex cost over $1 million to build and was generally considered the greatest of all interurban terminals. The gates across the tracks proved to be both expensive and unwieldy to operate and maintain. They were removed a few years after the visit of the trolley pilgrims. W.H. BASS PHOTO CO.

Members of the Board of Trade gave the trolley pilgrims a good send-off. By this time, car 502 had been liberally stocked with gifts of a certain product made famous by Kentucky. Obviously, the trolley pilgrims would not be thirsty on the next leg of their trip. It was also obvious that the Utica group and the Louisville group had enjoyed each other's company and would have preferred to prolong the visit.

Promptly at 2 p.m. car 502 with the Uticans on board left Louisville and crossed the Ohio River. George L. Danforth, chairman of the reception committee, and Edwin M. Babbitt, vice president and superintendent of the Rugby Distillery, accompanied the trolley pilgrims across the river and saw them safely on their way.

The return to Indianapolis followed the same route north as was used coming south. For the first 14 miles from Louisville to Sellersburg, car 502 traveled over the Louisville & Northern Railway. At Sellersburg, the 1,200-volt D.C. overhead was again encountered and car 502 had to be towed the 41 miles to Seymour by an Indianapolis & Louisville car. Once at Seymour, car 502 was able to operate on its own again and traveled the remaining 62 miles over the tracks of the Indianapolis, Columbus & Southern Traction Company.

Car 502 and the trolley pilgrims arrived in Indianapolis at about 6 p.m. They went directly to the Claypool Hotel which is where they had stayed when they passed through Indianapolis previously. Members of the Indianapolis Trade Association were waiting at the Claypool to welcome the Uticans to their fair city. They invited the trolley pilgrims to go on an automobile tour of Indianapolis on Wednesday morning.

Also at the Claypool awaiting the group was a familiar face. Manager C. Loomis Allen had returned to join the group after five days' absence.

Tuesday evening was spent sightseeing in the central part of Indianapolis. Noted by the Uticans was the Soldiers' and Sailors' Monument and fountain which was located in a circle in the center of the city. It reportedly had cost $600,000 to construct. The Uticans were impressed by the special lighting in the

Indiana Union Traction Company operated some very handsome and traditional wooden interurban cars in the 1910 era. Shown is IUT car 274 operating as the "Marion Flyer" between Indianapolis and Marion. W.H. BASS PHOTO CO.

The private parlor car *Lawton,* which undoubtedly was used by C.D. Emmons of the Fort Wayne & Wabash Valley Traction Company to reach Peru to meet the trolley pilgrims. McGRAW HILL PUBLISHING CO. FROM BRADLEY-HARNISH COLLECTION.

central business district that permitted people to walk the avenues and look at window displays until after midnight.

Wednesday, May 18, 1910
Indianapolis to Fort Wayne

The Indianapolis Trade Association made good their promise and had a dozen autos waiting in front of the Claypool Hotel early on Wednesday morning. As a matter of local pride, all of the autos had been made in Indianapolis and most were Overlands. Time was limited so the group kept a brisk pace and covered 25 miles on their brief sightseeing trip.

First, they visited several Indianapolis parks. Next they stopped at the famous race track in Indianapolis. Here they saw two Marmon autos race at speeds that took them over a mile in 50 seconds. The Uticans were invited to ride in the racing cars but everyone respectfully declined. From the race track they went to visit the Indianapolis Brewing Company. Finally, the group inspected A.C. Atkins & Co., a very large establishment that made saws.

Arriving back in downtown Indianapolis, the trolley pilgrims boarded car 502. Also boarding were Motorman C.M. Taylor and Conductor L.L. Anthony of the Indiana Union Traction Company who would guide the car the 75 miles north to Peru.

Union Traction was the largest interurban in Indiana in 1910. It controlled most of the routes north and northeast of Indianapolis. As its name indicates, Union Traction was a unification of at least 15 smaller interurban lines. However, the Union Traction itself had built the Indianapolis-Kokomo segment in 1903 and the Kokomo-Peru segment in 1904. The company had substantial passenger cars and operated through service in conjunction with the Fort Wayne & Wabash Valley Traction Company and would do so with the Winona Railroad in the future.

Leaving downtown Indianapolis at 10 a.m., car 502 followed the College streetcar line north and entered the tracks of the Indiana Union Traction Company on the north side of the city. Motorman George Moore and Conductor John O'Hara said that the line was well ballasted and well equipped. They were easily able to make their schedule. Motorman Taylor and Conductor Anthony of Union Traction offered some information on the company.

Indiana Union Traction Company had a total of 350 miles of road. Car 502 was operating over what was known as the Tipton Division. Arthur Brady was president and H.A. Nicholl was general manager.

After 56 miles of travel, Kokomo was reached at noon. Car 502 entered Kokomo going north on Union and stopped at the interurban stations near Sycamore. Kokomo was one of the smaller communities on the tour and the local residents and businessmen were excited about being included in the itinerary. At least two articles explaining about the Utica group and their tour were published in the Kokomo newspaper prior to their arrival.

A large group of businessmen and residents were waiting to welcome the trolley pilgrims to Kokomo. Included was a delegation from the Kokomo Manufacturers' and Merchants' Association, members of the Kokomo Improvement Association and representatives from other industrial, commercial and civic bodies. Following a cordial welcome and introductions, the trolley pilgrims were ushered aboard a special car of the Kokomo, Marion & Western Traction Company. This company ran the interurban line from Kokomo to Marion as well as the local streetcar lines in Kokomo. The private car carried the trolley pilgrims and some of their hosts on a brief trolley sightseeing tour of the city.

Upon returning to downtown, the trolley pilgrims left their sightseeing car and were escorted to the Hotel Francis where a luncheon had been set in their honor. Discussion during the meal covered both questions regarding Kokomo and the lengthy trip of the Uticans. It is interesting to note that the trolley pilgrims remembered Kokomo because Indiana had a county option law and the county around Kokomo did not permit the sale of intoxicating beverages. It was the first time that many of the Uticans had ever been in a prohibition county.

Leaving Kokomo at 1:30 p.m., car 502 and the trolley pilgrims headed north over Wabash Avenue to the Union Traction line to cover the 19 miles to Peru. Arriving, car 502 crossed a large bridge over the Wabash River and entered Peru on the Broadway streetcar line of the Fort Wayne & Wabash Valley Traction Company.

Peru was a major connection point for Union Traction. There were two routes between Indianapolis and Fort Wayne that were jointly operated by Union Traction and the Fort Wayne & Wabash Valley Traction Company. One route operated through Bluffton and the other route operated through Peru. Only three months earlier (February of 1910), the Winona Interurban Railway Co. had completed their link with the northern Indiana interurbans and Chicago. When car 502 arrived in Peru, Winona Lines was already operating through service from Peru to Goshen. By the end of the year, Winona Lines would be operating through service from Peru to Michigan City in conjunction with the Chicago, South Bend & Northern Indiana Railway, and through service from Indianapolis to Goshen via Peru in conjunction with Union Traction.

Only a brief stop was made at Peru to change pilot crews. The representatives from Union Traction left at this time as they had reached the end of Union Traction trackage. They were replaced by C.D. Emmons, general manager of the Fort Wayne & Wabash Valley Traction Company. Mr. Emmons had come from Fort Wayne in his private car to meet the trolley pilgrims and he took Manager Allen on board.[10]

The Fort Wayne & Wabash Valley Traction Company operated a 114-mile line along the Wabash River from Lafayette to Fort Wayne via Logansport, Peru and Wabash. It also operated a 25-mile line south from Fort Wayne to Bluffton. The line between Peru and Wabash was completed in 1901 and the line between Wabash and Fort Wayne was completed in 1902.

Car 502 left Peru on the East Main streetcar line and soon entered the Fort Wayne & Wabash Valley Traction Company interurban track going east. The track followed the Wabash River and its valley for the 59 miles to Fort Wayne. Car 502 entered Fort Wayne on the Taylor line of the local street railway.

The Longest Interurban Charter •

Fort Wayne & Wabash Valley Traction Company parlor-buffet car 501 was photographed while loading at Huntington, Indiana in 1906 or 1907. Four of these 61-foot cars were originally built for the 135-mile Indianapolis-Fort Wayne run. BRADLEY-HARNISH COLLECTION.

Fort Wayne & Wabash Valley Traction Company car 320 was photographed eastbound at Huntington, Indiana. This was one of three 63-foot wooden passenger cars built at the company's Fort Wayne shops. BRADLEY-HARNISH COLLECTION.

Ohio Electric Railway car 84 was photographed at Tillmans, east of Fort Wayne, Indiana. The car was westbound and was slowing down for the Fort Wayne & Findley Railroad crossing. BRADLEY-HARNISH COLLECTION.

The trolley pilgrims arrived in Fort Wayne at 5 p.m. and were welcomed by a large delegation from the Fort Wayne Commercial Club and Mayor Jesse L. Grice. A lengthy evening automobile tour of Fort Wayne had been arranged. Both manufacturing and the fine residential areas of the city were viewed. Later that night, the trolley pilgrims retired to the Hotel Anthony.

Fortunately, none of the participants that evening in Fort Wayne had a crystal ball because it would have put a severe damper on festivities. Only four months in the future, the Fort Wayne & Wabash Valley Traction Company would have a serious head-on collision of two trains south of Fort Wayne at Kingsland that would kill 41 passengers. This was the worst interurban wreck of all time and forced the FW&WV into bankruptcy followed by a reorganization as the Fort Wayne & Northern Indiana Traction Company.

Thursday, May 19, 1910
Fort Wayne to Toledo

On Thursday morning the trolley pilgrims had time to do a little sightseeing in Fort Wayne. Their first stop was at the store of Pixley & Co. from Utica. Here they were cordially received by Manager Stellhold. After this they visited several public buildings and places.

Car 502 left Fort Wayne at 10:30 a.m. via the Lewis streetcar line and entered the trackage of the Fort Wayne, Van Wert & Lima Traction Company for the 65 mile run to Lima, Ohio. On board and serving as pilot was F.A. Burkhardt, district passenger and freight agent of the Ohio Electric Railway. The Fort Wayne, Van Wert & Lima Traction Company began service between Fort Wayne and Lima in 1905. The company was leased by the Lima & Toledo Traction Company in 1906, which, in turn, became a part of the Ohio Electric Railway in 1907. Private right-of-way was used, generally adjacent to the Pennsylvania Railroad, except in major communities. This was considered a relatively fast line and used larger passenger cars. It was the second most important of the three links between the Indiana and Ohio interurban networks.

At about 12:40 p.m., car 502 entered Lima over the Grand and Main streetcar tracks of the Lima Electric Railway and Light Co. which was also controlled by the Ohio Electric Railway at this time. The trolley pilgrims were welcomed by Lima's Mayor Dyer and a large delegation from the Lima Progressive Association. They immediately retired to the Hotel Norval for a luncheon. Following this, the trolley pilgrims were taken on an hour tour of Lima by automobile.

Lima was a major junction point between competing interurban lines. At this time the Ohio Electric Railway controlled lines north to Toledo and south to Dayton and Cincinnati. The Western Ohio Railway also passed through Lima, and interlined with other companies to also provide service to Toledo and Dayton under the "Lima Route" banner.

In retrospect, the quickest and easiest route to Toledo would have seen car 502 remain on the Ohio Electric Railway and run north on its new (1908) Lima-Toledo line. However, Manager C. Loomis Allen had

Interurban Lines In The Toledo Area

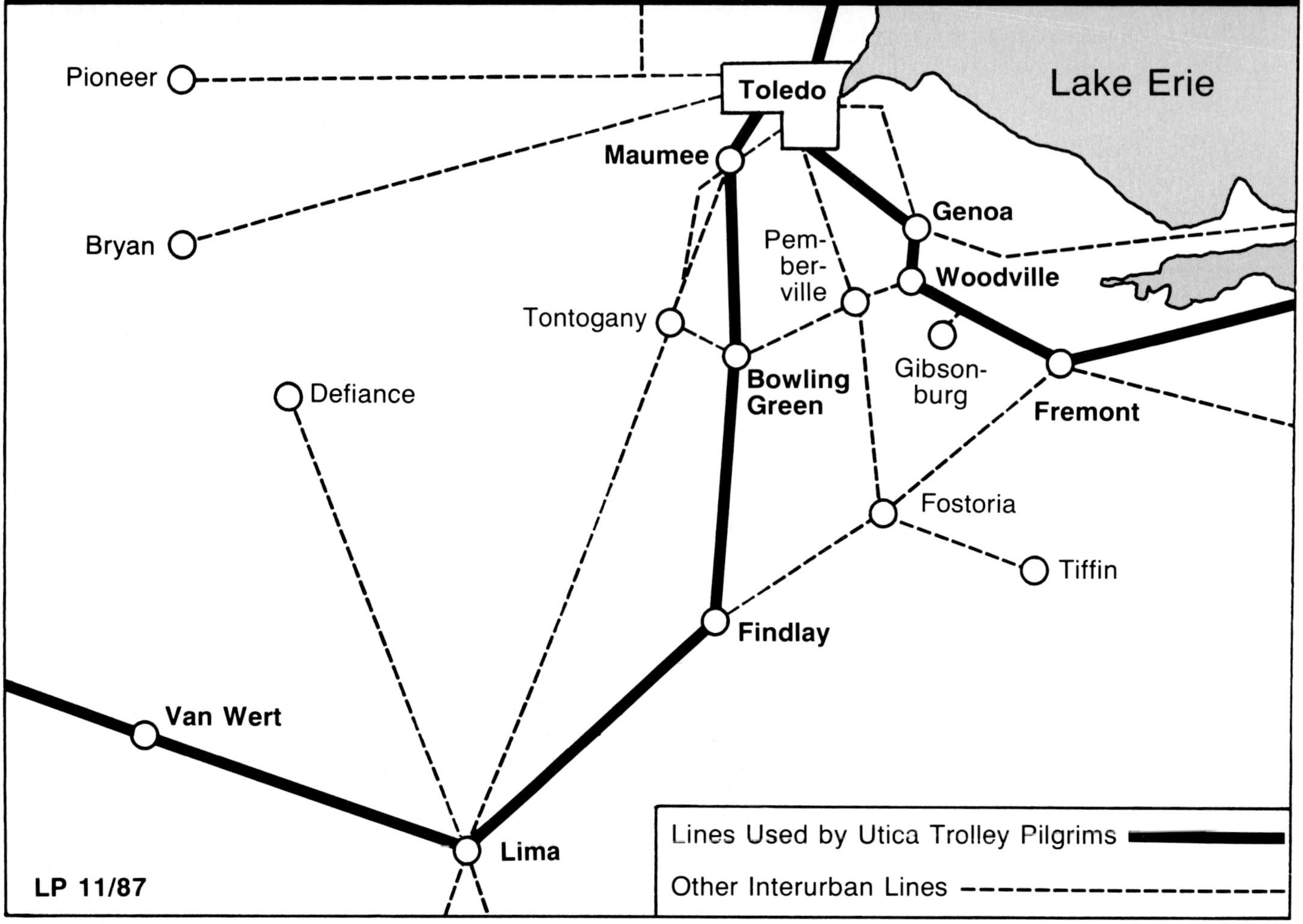

Western Ohio Railway car 17 poses with its crew. The white flags and "special" sign suggest a charter or some other special occasion. Note the sign on the front of the car that indicates the through "Lima Route" service from Toledo to Dayton via Findlay, Lima and Troy. DAVID SCHAFER COLLECTION.

The motorman and conductor of Toledo, Bowling Green & Southern car 120, a 45-foot single end car built in 1902, pose for the photographer with their car. The destination sign indicates that the car was on a local run from Toledo to Findlay. That huge pilot on the front of the car was a Toledo requirement and was designed to scoop up any pedestrian that accidentally strayed in front of a moving car. The sign on the pilot advertised a coming chautauqua event. M.D. McCARTER COLLECTION.

other ideas and routed car 502 over the longer "Lima Route" lines. Surviving documents contain no reason for this routing since no stops were recorded between Lima and Toledo.

After lunch, the trolley pilgrims returned to car 502 and found C.C. Collins, the traffic manager of the Lima-Findlay division of the Western Ohio Railway waiting for them. Mr. Collins would be their pilot over the Western Ohio tracks to Findlay.

Leaving Lima at about 3 p.m., car 502 operated north on Main Street and turned east on Robb and Keith to enter the trackage of the Western Ohio Railway. The Western Ohio was one of the larger interurbans and operated approximately 110 miles of line in 1910. The main line extended from Findlay through Lima and on south through Wapakoneta to Piqua. In addition, the company operated two branch lines west of Wapakoneta. The line between Lima and Findlay was opened in 1905 and was a major event since it was the line that completed the link between Dayton and Toledo. Soon afterwards, the Western Ohio participated in the "Lima Route" through service between Toledo and Dayton in conjunction with the Toledo, Bowling Green & Southern (Findlay-Toledo) and the Dayton & Troy (Piqua-Dayton). In later years the Lima-Findlay route would also see through service to Cleveland via two short connecting lines and the Lake Shore Electric beyond Fremont.

After 33 miles of travel from Lima, car 502 reached Findlay. Here it followed the same route as through cars of the "Lima Route" by operating over the Findlay Street Railway and turning north to the tracks of the Toledo, Bowling Green and Southern Traction Company. The TBG&S operated the 51 miles to Toledo via Bowling Green and had somewhat marginal trackage.

The Toledo, Bowling Green & Southern was a new name for an older line that had started through service from Findlay to Toledo in 1902. The company ran short cars that were not up to the standards of larger companies, and had a reputation for a poor right-of-way. However, the company did pool equipment with the Western Ohio and the Dayton & Troy on the through "Lima Route" service from Toledo to Lima and Dayton.

A major feature on this line was an 1,800-foot bridge over the Maumee River at Perrysburg. Entry to Toledo was over shared tracks with the Maumee Valley Railways & Light Co. and then over the South Detroit Avenue route of Toledo Railways & Light Co.

Car 502 and the trolley pilgrims arrived in Toledo at 7 p.m. The group then checked into the Hotel Secor where they were to spend the night. At the hotel they were met by a number of representatives of the Toledo Chamber of Commerce and an informal reception was held in the lobby of the hotel. The discussion included the details of a brief automobile tour of Toledo planned for the following morning. Several former Utica

The Longest Interurban Charter • **65**

Detroit, Monroe & Toledo Short Line car 517 pauses at the South Rockwood station in March of 1906. During this same month the company was absorbed into the Detroit United Lines. M.D. McCARTER COLLECTION.

Lake Shore Electric car 69 seated 42 passengers and was built by the J.G. Brill Co. in 1903. When new, it ran limited service between Toledo and Cleveland in 4½ hours. FOLLETT HOUSE MUSEUM.

residents also met and welcomed the trolley pilgrims upon their arrival.

Friday, May 20, 1910
Toledo to Detroit

It was raining in Toledo on Friday morning but the Toledo businessmen wanted the trolley pilgrims to see the city before their departure. Hence, several automobiles were lined up in front of the Hotel Secor at 9 a.m. to provide a tour this morning. The trolley pilgrims visited several places of interest including schools, parks and playgrounds.

After this they returned to downtown Toledo and the Uticans boarded car 502 to continue their journey. Mr. D.E. Lisle of the Detroit United Lines also came on board in order to guide the group north towards Detroit. Dr. Bierdemann, a former resident of Utica, accompanied them for part of the distance.

At 10:30 a.m., car 502 headed north from Toledo on rails that were part of the Detroit United Railway system. Known as the Detroit, Monroe & Toledo Short Line Railway, this company operated 56 miles from Toledo to Detroit. It was reportedly one of the best built lines in the Midwest. It was a relatively important line since it provided a connection with Detroit and the Michigan interurbans for several interurban lines that terminated at Toledo.

The Detroit, Monroe & Toledo Short Line was the only interurban link between Toledo and Detroit. Eight other interurbans reached Toledo, and four other interurban lines reached Detroit. Through service had started in 1904 after the Everett-Moore Syndicate had acquired the line from Toledo to Monroe and built the additional 36 miles into Detroit. The line was mostly on private right-of-way and substantially built with 70 pound rail, no major grades, no restricting curves, no grade crossings with other railroads and about half the distance was double tracked. It was reported that the line was quite profitable at this time.

Near Detroit, car 502 stopped and A.D.B. Van Zandt boarded. He was the publicity agent of Detroit United Lines and would accompany the car the remaining distance into Detroit. Car 502 pulled up to Detroit's Hotel Pontchartrain at 12:30 p.m.

At Detroit, the trolley pilgrims were very cordially welcomed by a delegation from the Detroit Board of Commerce. Several automobiles were waiting and the Uticans were soon whisked away for a tour of Detroit.

The first stop was at Belle Isle Park. Here, a fine luncheon was served in the park casino. A.D.B. Van Zandt together with John F. Key, general passenger agent and George W. Parker, general express agent, represented Detroit United Lines at the luncheon. At 3:30 p.m. the group returned to the automobiles to continue their tour of Detroit. Several hours were spent in riding through parks and over 14 miles of boulevard, viewing automobile plants, schools and buildings.

In Detroit, the trolley pilgrims were welcomed by another group from Utica. They had come to Detroit to check on the Gunn motor which had been invented by a Utican and had potential application in automobiles. It appears that the motor never reached practical production. Friday evening was spent in Detroit's Pontchartrain Hotel.

Saturday, May 21, 1910
Detroit to Cleveland

Saturday morning was a major turning point for the trolley pilgrims. It effectively marked the end of the tour and changing direction to head for home. With the exception of luncheon stops and a proposed evening tour of Buffalo, the civic activities of the tour ended at Detroit. Reports on the actions of the trolley pilgrims were extremely meager on these last three days. From a practical standpoint, it no longer became necessary to send letters and reports back home since the trolley pilgrims would arrive at the same time as a letter. It is also easy to imagine that the trolley pilgrims were exhausted from their travels and had more interest in going home than in exploring more cities.

Edward J. Wright, superintendent of the Oneida Railway, took over as transportation chairman of car 502 as they left Detroit. He had earlier ridden with the group at the start of the trip from Utica to Rochester. It appears that C. Loomis Allen had left the group in Detroit to run ahead to the Cleveland area where he had been employed years previously.

Herman Reichert and E.D. Rich of the Detroit Board of Commerce wanted to take the trolley pilgrims to Ann Arbor on Saturday morning. No report survives as to whether this tour was taken but it is unlikely given the amount of travel and departure time on Saturday.

Car 502 left Detroit at 10 a.m. and operated south, retracing its route on the Detroit United's Detroit, Monroe & Toledo Short Line Railway the 56 miles to Toledo. Surviving records suggest that the trolley pilgrims reached Toledo about noon, but that no stop was made. At Toledo, car 502 entered the trackage of the highly respected Lake Shore Electric for the run to Cleveland.

The only substantial stop scheduled for Saturday was planned at Fremont, Ohio, about 33 miles beyond Toledo. Car 502 and the trolley pilgrims reached Fremont a few minutes after 1 p.m. They were welcomed to Fremont by a small group of businessmen led by Mr. M. Gusdorf, secretary of the Fremont Municipal Association. Mr. Gusdorf escorted the trolley pilgrims to the Hotel Fremont where lunch was served.

Following lunch, the Uticans were introduced to several Fremont businessmen and bankers. The introductions were followed by a brief 30-minute automobile tour of Fremont using at least eight vehicles. The itinerary of the tour included the west end factory district out West State Street and Spiegel Grove, the site of the Rutherford B. Hayes home. Following a tour of other sections of the community, the automobiles returned on Front Street to downtown and back to car 502. Bidding farewell to their Fremont hosts, the trolley pilgrims departed at 2:30 p.m., their scheduled departure time.

The Lake Shore Electric was one of the larger, better-known and more prosperous interurbans in the Midwest. It was created by the Everett-Moore Syndicate in 1901 by merging several smaller interurbans between Cleveland and Toledo. Through service into Detroit over the Detroit United had not yet started in 1910. Hence, car 502 and the trolley pilgrims accounted for one of the earlier through runs of a passenger car between Detroit and Cleveland.

A Cleveland, Painesville & Eastern car crosses the big interurban bridge near Willoughby. The photo was taken from a postcard dated July 21, 1910. DAVID SCHAFER COLLECTION.

Conneaut & Erie Traction Co. car 3 was photographed while on a run to Conneaut. The third member of the crew may have handled the express in the compartment on the rear of the car. This photo dates prior to 1909, the year that the Conneaut & Erie Traction Company became the Cleveland & Erie Railway. DAVID SCHAFER COLLECTION.

Between Fremont and Ceylon Junction (located between Huron and Vermilon) the Lake Shore Electric had two routes. The original and longer route went somewhat south via Norwalk. A newer route was opened in 1907 via Sandusky. Car 502 and the trolley pilgrims used the newer and shorter route via Sandusky. Nearing Vickery, 10 miles from Fremont, car 502 overtook a Lake Erie & Western (NYC&HR) local passenger train traveling in the same direction. The Uticans had no difficulty in leaving it behind amid the cheers of the passengers on both the steam train and car 502.

A brief stop was made at Lorain to pick up three passengers; C. Loomis Allen, D.W. Dean and J.J. Stanley. Allen briefly returned to the group. He was familiar with this area because he had formerly managed the line from Lorain to Elyria. Dean was connected with the J.G. Brill Company, which had built car 502 three years previously. He was interested in how the car was doing on such a long trip.

Stanley was known to some of the Uticans and had previously ridden with the trolley pilgrims from Rush Road to Cleveland. He managed the Utica Belt Line Street Railroad for two years after it was purchased by a Cleveland group and he was responsible for the electric rail extensions to Clinton, Rome and Little Falls. He had returned to Cleveland and currently served as president of Cleveland Railway which ran over 1,000 cars on 260 miles of track.

The 116-mile trip over the Lake Shore Electric between Toledo and Cleveland was the longest single segment of travel by the trolley pilgrims.

At Cleveland, C. Loomis Allen left the group once again. He went on ahead to make sure that suitable arrangements had been made for a welcome in Utica. The trolley pilgrims again spent the night at the Hollenden Hotel. This was only the second time on the trip that they had spent two nights in the same hotel. The other instance was the Claypool Hotel in Indianapolis.

Sunday, May 22, 1910
Cleveland to Buffalo

An early start was planned on Sunday since the trolley pilgrims had many miles to cover. Joseph Jordan, general manager of the Cleveland, Painesville & Eastern Railroad, boarded car 502 on Sunday morning to pilot the group as far as Ashtabula.

An 8 a.m. start had originally been planned. However, the departure time came and went before the luggage had arrived at the car. The problem was eventually resolved but car 502 was 20 minutes late when it finally got underway. From Cleveland, the group headed east and retraced the same route they had followed west 10 days earlier. Although the delay in leaving Cleveland was minor, it soon created major problems for the group and their proposed schedule. The delay was sufficient to make the initially planned meets with other cars impossible. Hence, car 502 was held back and assigned different sidings and times for meets. The group got later and later as the day wore on.

At Ashtabula, a brief stop was made to change pilots. Mr. Jordan left and was replaced by Palmer Wardman, general superintendent of the Pennsylvania & Ohio. Car 502 then continued east over P&O trackage.

Both eastbound and westbound, the trolley pilgrims spent their night in Cleveland at the Hollenden Hotel. This photo from that period was taken from an old postcard. DAVID SCHAFER COLLECTION.

Another stop was made at Conneaut to change pilots. R.W. Palmer, general manager of the Cleveland & Erie Railway, boarded the car to guide it to Erie. To their dismay, the trolley pilgrims found that another change was necessary at Conneaut. They had entered the eastern time zone and found it necessary to set their watches ahead an hour, making their lateness seem even worse.

Erie was finally reached at 3 p.m. and a brief stop was called for a late lunch. In spite of their late arrival, several Erie businessmen were awaiting the appearance of the Uticans. They were also met by Matthew C. Brush, general manager of the Buffalo & Lake Erie Traction Company, who had accompanied the trolley pilgrims on their westbound trip. During lunch at the Reed House, the Erie businessmen suggested that the Uticans remain in Erie until the following morning in order to see more of their city. However, the trolley pilgrims, undoubtedly happy to be heading home, declined the offer and continued on their way after lunch accompanied by Mr. Brush.

Soon after leaving Erie, a stop was made to pick up George M. Brush, the traffic manager of the Buffalo & Lake Erie Traction and father of the general manager. At least two delays were encountered between Erie and Buffalo. At one location a new pavement was being put down and the track was temporarily impassable. Mr. Brush and his assistants made a major effort and got car 502 rolling again.

Records indicate that the trolley pilgrims were apprehensive about clearing the Nickel Plate bridge at Farnham once again. Later reports indicate that the main track under the bridge had been lowered to ease the passage of car 502.

This photo looks west and shows the viaduct in Farnham, New York that carried the Nickel Plate and Pennsylvania Railroad tracks over the Buffalo & Lake Erie Traction Company. The photo was taken in 1910 or 1911 and shows that the main line track (left) was lowered through the underpass as a result of the clearance problem of car 502 and the Utica Electric Railway Tour on May 11, 1910. J.R. McFARLANE COLLECTION.

Buffalo, Lockport & Rochester car 215 was built in 1908 by the Niles Car Company and was one of the initial order of cars when the line opened. This photo was taken after 1919, when the company name was changed to the Rochester, Lockport & Buffalo Railroad Company. SHELDEN S. KING COLLECTION.

The arrival at Buffalo had originally been scheduled for 6:30 p.m. A delegation from the Buffalo Chamber of Commerce & Manufacturers' Club had planned to give the trolley pilgrims an automobile tour of Buffalo as had been promised on the outbound trip. This was to be followed by dinner at the Buffalo Club. Unfortunately, the program was cancelled because the trolley pilgrims were delayed and did not arrive until 10:30 p.m. Even with their late arrival, a small group was still waiting to welcome them including J.A. Calish, vice president of the Buffalo & Lake Erie Traction Company.

Sunday night was spent in the Lafayette Hotel in Buffalo.

Monday, May 23, 1910
Buffalo to Utica

The trolley pilgrims left Buffalo at 9 a.m. on Monday on the last day of their journey. W.T. Higley, superintendent of transportation for the Buffalo, Lockport & Rochester Railway, boarded car 502 at Buffalo to act as pilot. It is interesting that the International Railway did not supply a pilot as the BL&R passenger trains did not normally operate over IRC tracks at this time. Going east, they followed the same route they had used going west.

On the way to Rochester, a stop was made to pick up a number of electric railway officials. This was the first group to welcome the trolley pilgrims back home. Boarding were E.J. Cook, vice president and general manager of the New York State Railways, Rochester Lines, and several associates including B.E. Wilson, general passenger agent and D.F. Beach, company attorney. Also joining the group at this time were J.M. Campbell, general manager, and John H. Cain, superintendent of the Buffalo, Lockport & Rochester Railway. It might be remembered that John Cain had been involved with installing the new crossing on the west side of Rochester. Several of these electric railway officials expressed substantial interest in the nearly-completed trip of the trolley pilgrims and asked many questions.

Approaching Rochester, the trolley pilgrims were delighted to find that there was no delay or problem in crossing the New York Central tracks at Otis station. The temporary crossing, put in nearly two weeks previously, had now been made permanent. A brief lunch stop was made in Rochester. Vice President Cook of New York State Railways provided a luncheon for everyone at the Powers Hotel. Following lunch, the trolley pilgrims boarded car 502 for what may have been the last time as they started the last leg of their journey home. In their haste, the car actually began running a few minutes ahead of schedule.

Meanwhile, as car 502 rolled east, Utica was preparing for the arrival of the trolley pilgrims.

During the trip, reports on the activities of the trolley pilgrims and letters to their families had reached Utica. The group, the trip and their activities were the most popular subject in Utica at this time. Reports were published in the newspapers and the trolley pilgrims grabbed the attention of Utica residents in a fashion similar to latter-day rocket launchings and space pioneers.

Plans for a return welcome and celebration were being made at least a week in advance. A Welcoming Committee in Utica was appointed and had its first meeting on the evening of Monday, May 16. The meeting was held in the rooms of the Utica Chamber of Commerce and was chaired by Charles W. Wicks.

It was decided to hold a banquet at Bagg's Hotel for the trolley pilgrims on the evening of their return. Those wishing to join the group at the banquet would be charged $10 and would also be given transportation to Syracuse on chartered cars of the Oneida Railway to welcome the trolley pilgrims upon their arrival at that point. There would be room on the cars for those wishing to go to Syracuse but not participate in the banquet.

Other welcoming activities included a parade into town with a brass band and automobiles provided by the Utica Automobile Club.

Like most everything else associated with the trip, the welcoming celebration went well and exactly as planned.

At 2:05 p.m. on Monday afternoon, May 23, two chartered cars of the Oneida Railway left Utica for Syracuse. In charge of the special trip for the delegation was C.R. Gowen, general passenger agent of the Oneida Railway. John Bonn was the conductor and John Hall and John North were the motormen. Two motormen were required because the two cars left Utica individually and were coupled into a two-car train when they left city streets and entered West Shore tracks. On board were 79 prominent citizens of Utica who constituted the banquet group and the early welcoming delegation. George Hotaling, chief dispatcher for the Oneida Railway also came along. They arrived at Syracuse at 3:30 p.m. and awaited the arrival of the trolley pilgrims from the west.

Car 502 and the trolley pilgrims reached the electric terminal station in Syracuse at 4:15 p.m., having paused briefly outside the station to adjust the third rail shoes. When they pulled in, they were immediately welcomed back from their trip by the Uticans in the two chartered cars. Since the Oneida Railway cars had multiple unit capabilities, the two cars of welcomers were coupled behind car 502 after they left the streets at the Syracuse city line. Now a three-car train, it continued east to Utica. Manager C. Loomis Allen once again joined the group and stepped to the front of car 502 and took over as motorman to guide the trolley pilgrims on the last segment of their journey. It is reported that Allen wasted no time going east and nearly set a record reaching Utica.

At 5:45 p.m. the trolley pilgrims and the three-car train left the West Shore tracks on the south side of Utica. As the train entered Genesee Street, the passengers found a substantial welcome and parade waiting for them. Car 502 was once again decorated with a large flag. Bergner's Band led the parade riding on an open trolley car. Behind the band was the motorcycle parade of the Utica Police Department followed by Commissioner of Safety Foley and Chief Coakley. Then came the electric cars with the trolley pilgrims and the early welcoming delegation. At the rear of the parade were 76 automobiles.

The final distance down Genesee Street to Bagg's Square was covered very slowly and with a great deal

Rochester, Syracuse & Eastern car 127 was photographed westbound at the Winton Road stop. This location is now within the City of Rochester and the interurban right-of-way is now University Avenue. SHELDEN S. KING COLLECTION.

Car 518 trails a westbound Oneida Railway two-car train at the Canastota station in about 1910. A fence prevented passengers from crossing the tracks even though the third rail had a protective wood covering on the top and two sides. The signal rods in the left foreground were operated from a tower in the distance and controlled a crossing with the Lehigh Valley Railroad, behind the cameraman. J.R. McFARLANE COLLECTION.

The triumphant return of the trolley pilgrims to Utica on Monday, May 23, 1910. Car 502 heads the three-car train down Genesee Street in the parade while crowds watch from the curb. Reproduced from a 1910 newspaper clipping in the Utica scrapbook. ONEIDA COUNTY HISTORICAL SOCIETY.

of noise. Motormen on the electric cars started tooting their whistles and even a steam locomotive engineer at the South Utica station joined in. Utica residents lined both sides of Genesee Street and loudly welcomed the trolley pilgrims home. Several had horns, whistles and other noisemakers. The children at the House of the Good Shepherd and Utica Orphan Asylum, as well as the nurses at the hospital and many business people stood waving flags. Many of the stores along the route had been specially decorated for this occasion. Even the City Hall was trimmed with flags. The parade finally reached Bagg's Hotel at 6:20 p.m.

Following the parade, the trolley pilgrims were escorted into Bagg's Hotel for a banquet. Although scheduled to start at 7 p.m., the welcomes and handshaking delayed the start of activities by 30 minutes. Veteran Conductor John O'Hara and Motorman George Moore, who had been with the trolley pilgrims for the past two weeks, were included in the banquet group. W.I. Tabor, president of the Chamber of Commerce presided and introduced George E. Dunham as toastmaster. Hon. William Townsend and Hon. F.M. Calder delivered addresses of welcome to the trolley pilgrims. Expectedly, C. Loomis Allen was cheered and toasted. The banquet continued until 10:45 p.m. as the trolley pilgrims told of their observations and exploits on their tour.

As an interesting end to the day's activities, car 502 was once again taken out on the line. At 11:30 p.m. the car left Utica and went east on the Utica & Mohawk Valley line to Little Falls. This was the eastern end of the Midwest interurban network and the location the car started from on May 9. After that the car returned to Utica. Later, after the car's interior was restored to normal use, each of the trolley pilgrims was given one of the wicker chairs as a memento.

There is no question that the trip was an unqualified success from virtually every standpoint. The Uticans were able to visit branches of several Utica businesses. They also acquired a great deal of information on taxes, utilities, and civic improvements in the communities visited. Most of this information is very interesting and historical but has not been included here because of space limitations and because it did not directly pertain to the electric railway network.

In addition, the trip obviously brought fame to Utica and enhanced its reputation. A trail of Utica Booster buttons was left behind and Utica received much publicity in local newspapers. Many of the civic organizations along the route paid Utica the ultimate compliment by saying they wished they had thought of taking the trip first. Wherever they went, the trolley pilgrims left an image of Utica that indicated an interest in business, an interest in civic improvement and a willingness to pioneer new ideas.

At the same time, the trip had positive effects for both the Oneida Railway and the interurban industry in general. Reports of the trip appeared in the trade press and enhanced the reputation of C. Loomis Allen and the Oneida Railway. Interurban companies along the route received a great deal of favorable publicity in local newspapers.

Perhaps above all else, the trip proved the compatibility of the interurban network. The concept of a trip of this magnitude is almost mind-boggling. The fact that it was accomplished virtually on schedule and with no major problems is a credit to the planning of C. Loomis Allen and the reliability of the equipment, personnel and trackage of this period. In spite of the many builders, lines and original specifications involved, it did prove that the interurbans were much more compatible and similar in design and operation than many had believed.

Regardless of the accomplishments, the trip was undoubtedly unique. Who among us would not have paid dearly for a seat on Oneida Railway car 502 in May of 1910 and for this opportunity to view the interurban network at its prime?

4

Records and Accomplishments

The trip of the Utica trolley pilgrims deserves a place in history similar to countless other sagas that are subject to continued research and interpretation. On several occasions it seemed that each new item of information uncovered regarding the trip only created another question.

In particular, the trip by the Utica businessmen was an ideal use of a long-distance chartered interurban car. One wonders which came first, the purpose of this trip or the concept of long distance travel by interurban. A review of the route and planning brings up questions but also engenders some admiration for the planning ability of C. Loomis Allen. We would like to have the opportunity of going back in time to interview Mr. Allen and obtain answers to some of these questions. Short of that, it would have been helpful to place a knowledgeable individual on car 502 to faithfully document this trip. Since neither alternative is available, we are left with doing the best we can with the resources available.

Following are some of the more important and interesting facts and data pertaining to this trip.

Records Set

This trip set the all-time record for the longest charter trip by interurban railway. Since there is no evidence to the contrary, it also set the record for longest continuous passenger travel by interurban and trolley on a single trip.

These records can be expanded slightly. At its peak, the electric interurban network far surpassed any network of electrified steam railroad trackage. Hence, this trip also set similar all-time distance records for all electric railway travel in North America.

PRECEDING PAGE

Car 502 is shown as it operated in regular service during the 1920s following a substantial overhaul at the start of that decade. This project included the installation of steel sheathing, modification for double end operation and replacement of the train doors by solid ends. ONEIDA COUNTY HISTORICAL SOCIETY.

In addition, this trip can claim one more record. It was responsible for the installation of the missing 80 feet of track in Rochester and was the first car and first passengers to use it. This apparently was the final track link that brought the Midwest interurban network to its fullest extent.

Interurban Lines Covered

A listing of interurban lines covered is supplied. The actual number involved with this trip is subject to individual interpretation.

There were a total of 43 different route segments involved in the trip. Fourteen of these were the same segments that were covered by car 502 in both directions and two were owned by the same company. Thus there were 28 different interurban lines covered.

From this point each individual can add or subtract depending on criteria selected. Addition is possible because some of the trackage used was technically owned by a subsidiary or affiliated company. Prime examples are the use of the Syracuse, Lake Shore & Northern trackage when entering Syracuse on the Rochester, Syracuse & Eastern; and the use of Buffalo & Lackawanna Traction Company trackage when entering Buffalo on the Buffalo & Lake Erie Traction Company.

Subtraction is possible due to similar ownership or operation. The Ohio Electric Railway was responsible for three segments of the trip. However, in all three cases the trackage used was owned by a different company that had been leased to the Ohio Electric. The Cleveland, Southwestern & Columbus was responsible for two unconnected segments of the trip, both built by different companies and part of different routes. In at least two cases, neighboring segments were technically owned by different companies but under the same control. Examples include the Cleveland, Painesville & Ashtabula Railroad with the Cleveland, Painesville & Eastern Railroad; and the Columbus, Marion & Bucyrus Railroad with the Columbus, Delaware & Marion Railway.

Regardless of the number of interurban companies used, it should be noted that car 502 also made use

The Longest Interurban Charter • 75

Interurban Lines Covered and Mileage

Cities	Interurban Line	Miles	Total
Little Falls-Utica	Utica & Mohawk Valley Railway	23	
	Total mileage for Monday, May 9, 1910		23
Utica-Syracuse	Oneida Railway	49	
Syracuse-Rochester	Rochester, Syracuse & Eastern Railroad[1]	86	
	Total mileage for Tuesday, May 10, 1910		135
Rochester-Lockport	Buffalo, Lockport & Rochester Railway	58	
Lockport-Buffalo	International Railway	25	
Buffalo-Erie	Buffalo & Lake Erie Traction Company[2]	93	
	Total mileage for Wednesday, May 11, 1910		176
Erie-Conneaut	Cleveland & Erie Railway	33	
Conneaut-Ashtabula	Pennsylvania & Ohio Railway	14	
Ashtabula-Painesville	Cleveland, Painesville & Ashtabula Railroad	27	
Painesville-Cleveland	Cleveland, Painesville & Eastern Railroad	30	
	Total mileage for Thursday, May 12, 1910		104
Cleveland-Norwalk	Cleveland, Southwestern & Columbus Railway	58	
Norwalk-Shelby	Sandusky, Norwalk & Mansfield Electric Railway	25	
Shelby-Mansfield	Mansfield Railway Light & Power Company	12	
Mansfield-Bucyrus	Cleveland Southwestern & Columbus Railway	29	
Bucyrus-Marion	Columbus, Marion & Bucyrus Railroad	18	
Marion-Columbus	Columbus, Delaware & Marion Railway	50	
	Total mileage for Friday, May 13, 1910		192
Columbus-Dayton	Ohio Electric Ry. (Indiana, Columbus & Eastern Traction Co.)	75	
	Total mileage for Saturday, May 14, 1910		75
Dayton-Richmond	Ohio Electric Ry. (Dayton & Western Traction Co.)	40	
Richmond-Indianapolis	Terre Haute, Indianapolis & Eastern Traction Company	69	
	Total mileage for Sunday, May 15, 1910		109
Indianapolis-Seymour	Indianapolis, Columbus & Southern Traction Company	62	
Seymour-Sellersburg	Indianapolis & Louisville Traction Company	41	
Sellersburg-Louisville	Louisville & Northern Railway & Lighting Company	14	
	Total mileage for Monday, May 16, 1910		117
Louisville-Sellersburg	Louisville & Northern Railway & Lighting Company	14	
Sellersburg-Seymour	Indianapolis & Louisville Traction Company	41	
Seymour-Indianapolis	Indianapolis, Columbus & Southern Traction Company	62	
	Total mileage for Tuesday, May 17, 1910		117
Indianapolis-Peru	Indiana Union Traction Company	75	
Peru-Fort Wayne	Fort Wayne & Wabash Valley Traction Company	59	
	Total mileage for Wednesday, May 18, 1910		134
Fort Wayne-Lima	Ohio Electric Ry. (Fort Wayne, Van Wert & Lima Traction Co.)	65	
Lima-Findlay	Western Ohio Railway	33	
Findlay-Toledo	Toledo, Bowling Green & Southern Traction Company	51	
	Total mileage for Thursday, May 19, 1910		149
Toledo-Detroit	Detroit United (Detroit, Monroe & Toledo Short Line Railway)	56	
	Total mileage for Friday, May 20, 1910		56
Detroit-Toledo	Detroit United (Detroit, Monroe & Toledo Short Line Railway)	56	
Toledo-Cleveland	Lake Shore Electric Railway[3]	116	
	Total mileage for Saturday, May 21, 1910		172
Cleveland-Painesville	Cleveland, Painesville & Eastern Railroad	30	
Painesville-Ashtabula	Cleveland, Painesville & Ashtabula Railroad	27	
Ashtabula-Conneaut	Pennsylvania & Ohio Railway	14	
Conneaut-Erie	Cleveland & Erie Railway	33	
Erie-Buffalo	Buffalo & Lake Erie Traction Company[2]	93	
	Total mileage for Sunday, May 22, 1910		197
Buffalo-Lockport	International Railway	25	
Lockport-Rochester	Buffalo, Lockport & Rochester Railway	58	
Rochester-Syracuse	Rochester, Syracuse & Eastern Railroad[1]	86	
Syracuse-Utica	Oneida Railway	49	
Utica-Little Falls	Utica & Mohawk Valley Railway	23	
	Total mileage for Monday, May 23, 1910		241
	Grand Total for Mileage		1997

1. Includes 4 miles over the Syracuse, Lake Shore & Northern. 2. Includes 5 miles over the Buffalo & Lackawanna Traction Company. 3. Mileage based on route via Sandusky.

September of 1922 finds car 502 in regular service about to depart from the electric railway terminal in Syracuse for a run to Utica. By this time the appearance of car 502 had changed substantially from the time of the 1910 trip and the Oneida Railway was now known as the Oneida Line of New York State Railways. J.R. McFARLANE COLLECTION.

of the trackage of numerous street railway companies in many cities. Some of these were owned or controlled by the interurbans (or the interubans were controlled by the street railway), while others were large, independent companies. No attempt has been made to count the street railways used on this trip but it is a significant number.

Distance Covered

It has also proven difficult to track down the exact mileage of this trip. It appears that no one on car 502 attempted to keep an accurate record of mileage. Most newspaper accounts of the trip failed to mention an exact figure and instead simply stated "nearly 2,000 miles" or "about 2,000 miles." One exception to this is a figure of 2,049.82 miles mentioned in a Dayton newspaper.[1] However, this figure was prepared by C. Loomis Allen for the initial proposed itinerary and includes the anticipated round trip to Cincinnati, which was mentioned later in the same article. It probably would have been impossible for the passengers to keep an accurate accounting of mileage even if they had tried. This car was not equipped with an odometer and some of the mileage information provided by the pilot crews and on-board visitors appears to be at least slightly inaccurate.

Attempting to reconstruct an accurate accounting of mileage some 78 years later proved to be no less of a problem. Mileage figures are available in historical books, old schedules and verbal comments recorded on car 502. In many cases the figures differed at least slightly.

The accompanying chart gives a listing of route segments and also provides a record of mileage based on available figures. In all cases, the lowest reliable figure was used. The total shows a distance of 1,997 miles. This is actually a minimum figure and is subject to revision for several reasons:

• The figures show downtown-to-downtown mileage for the interurbans. Nothing has been added for mileage to get to and from hotels or for side trips by electric railways. This would have involved extra mileage in Ashtabula, Dayton, Louisville and Kokomo.

• Over and above "live" mileage, it is known that car 502 accumulated some substantial "deadhead" miles on this trip to go to car barns for service or night storage. One record indicates that car 502 travelled 24 "deadhead" miles in the Dayton area for service.

• Finally, in spite of the efforts of C. Loomis Allen, the mileage between Utica and Little Falls is subject to question. Very few passengers rode this segment on May 9, and it is believed that none of the trolley pilgrims rode to Little Falls on the evening of May 23. Hence, this segment is applicable to car 502 but may not be applicable from the standpoint of commercial passengers.

Overall, it is probably safe to estimate total "live" distance at very close to 2,000 miles and total distance of car 502 at slightly above that.

Competing Trips and Alternate Routes

One would have thought that the Utica trip would have been followed by a number of imitators attempting to beat the record of the Utica businessmen and

C. Loomis Allen showed his wisdom by selecting the month of May for the Utica Electric Railway Tour. A tour two months earlier would have scheduled the trip in the spring flooding season while two months later would have scheduled it in the heat of summer. Had the trolley pilgrims elected to make their trip in the spring of 1913 they would have encountered this sight on the Lake Shore Electric in Fremont, Ohio. Flooding got so bad on the city streets that several interurban trains were stalled on the edge of town and this special "floodcar" was used to shuttle passengers over the deeper areas. HELEN M. HANSEN/FOLLETT HOUSE MUSEUM.

Some interurban lines were able to operate modern high-speed cars by the 1930s. This example was operated by the Indiana Railroad, a company that consolidated most of the interurban lines radiating from Indianapolis. A car of this type was the last passenger interurban to operate over the route of the trolley pilgrims when it was involved in an accident on the Indianapolis-Seymour line on September 8, 1941. LARRY PLACHNO COLLECTION.

claim fame for another city. Such was not the case. The one known example is that shortly after the Utica trip returned home, the Indianapolis Trade Association began planning a tour by interurban car to 32 towns and cities in northern Indiana. They planned to bring along a printing press so that they could provide literature as needed. But the overall mileage would have been small compared to the Utica tour. However, there were few charter trips with passengers that covered more than three or four lines. Almost none of these received the publicity that the Uticans obtained in 1910.

There are perhaps three reasons why the Utica trip was never duplicated. These include the nature of interurban travel, the time frame and the geographic limitations of the interurban network.

Nature of Interurban Travel

Interurbans were traditionally a local enterprise. The typical interurban passenger rode only a short distance — either from a rural stop to the city or between two nearby cities. Most interurbans were too slow to win any significant long distance passenger traffic away from the steam railroads. Very few of the interurbans had sufficient mileage or sufficient long distance passengers to warrant operating dining cars and only a very few companies attempted to operate sleeping cars. Passengers traveling between two distant points would elect to go by steam railroad because it was faster and often less expensive.

The only long distance travel that would have been viable by interurban was a tour whereby the group made multiple stops along the way and was in no hurry to get to their destination. The Utica trip fell within this criteria. As such it was virtually unique and very few trips had a similar need.

Timing

A second reason for the lack of duplicate trips was the timing. The Utica trip was operated at the most ideal time. By 1910, the interurban network had been almost totally completed and the industry was optimistic. Five years later, this aura of optimism would be gone and the threat of the automobile would be recognized. Ten years later, in 1920, some of the interurbans would be fighting for survival and a very definite and obvious downward trend would set in.

All of the lines covered by the Utica trip remained in operation at least into 1921. In that year, the Sandusky, Norwark & Mansfield de-electrified. However, a Cleveland to Columbus all-electric route would still have been possible on the Cleveland, Southwestern & Columbus via Seville. In 1922 the Cleveland & Erie was abandoned thus making it impossible to duplicate the Utica trip. The other Ohio and Indiana interurbans used by the Uticans did survive until about the 1930s.

The last segment of track used by the Utica trip to remain in operation as an electric passenger interurban was the line between Indianapolis and Seymour which was abandoned in 1941 following an accident between the only two cars on the line. Some local streetcar trackage used by car 502 remained in use until a later date.

Geographic Limitations

Finally, there is the question of whether a longer trip by interurban was even practical. The interesting, though somewhat qualified, answer is no.

Most of the route used by the Uticans was based on a large loop connecting Cleveland, Columbus, Dayton, Indianapolis, Fort Wayne, Toledo and back to Cleveland. As it turns out, this was the largest circle trip possible connecting major cities by interurban without retracing the route. One questions whether C. Loomis Allen knew this and intentionally set up the route this way. It was technically possible to increase this loop slightly (such as Indianapolis to Peru via Lebanon and Lafaytte) but that would not have added any major cities. As it was, the Uticans took the long way between Cleveland and Mansfield and the long way between Lima and Toledo. Once again, one wonders if this routing was intended by Allen to prevent a following trip from attaining the same distance.

The trolley pilgrims on the 1910 trip were aware that they were setting a new record in electric railway travel as that was mentioned by several newspapers. It is possible that Allen specifically set up his route to cover maximum miles and make it difficult for a later trip to exceed this distance.

Adding any more mileage to the Utica trip to reach major cities would have required retracing the route to get back to this big loop, would have added only one or two more major cities and might have encountered problems of incompatibility.

The most logical addition to the Utica tour would have been a side trip south from Dayton to the outskirts of Cincinnati. Surviving accounts indicate that this had originally been included in the itinerary for the trolley pilgrims but was omitted at a later date. (Two contemporary newspaper accounts and one current historical account do erroneously credit the 1910 Utica trip with including Cincinnati in the itinerary.) Unfortunately, a conventional interurban car would not have been able to operate in Cincinnati because of its dual overhead and wide gauge trackage. The car would have had to return to Dayton via the same trackage.

Another potential side trip could have seen a car go from Cleveland into the Akron-Canton-Youngstown area. Continuation to Pittsburgh would have been impossible since the connecting interurban had both the wrong track gauge and wrong voltage. Again, the car would have had to double back and return to Cleveland.

It was possible to go from Peru north to South Bend and Michigan City. Entry into Chicago by a conventional interurban car would have been difficult because of the high voltage alternating current power used by the Chicago, Lake Shore & South Bend. Again, the car would have had to return to Peru via the same trackage.

Interurban lines did extend beyond Detroit to Flint, Lansing, Battle Creek and Grand Rapids. Flint could have been a potential target for an electric railway trip. However, most of these other destinations were not practical because the connecting interurban lines had different voltages and third rail operation.

Finally, there were numerous side trips possible that did not involve large cities and required a return over the same route. These included Columbus-Zanesville, Indianapolis-Terre Haute and several others.

The Longest Interurban Charter • **79**

Car 502 was photographed while eastbound on Burnet Avenue in Syracuse on a regular trip from Syracuse to Utica. This photo was taken on a snowy day in December of 1930, the last month of operation for the Oneida Line of New York State Railways. The last revenue run ended about an hour into the new year. J.R. McFARLANE COLLECTION.

Car 502 was photographed adjacent to the Wolf Street Shops in Syracuse. The actual date of the photo is not known. However, it appears that the photo was taken during the 1920s since car 502 had already been overhauled but seems to still be in revenue passenger service. ONEIDA COUNTY HISTORICAL SOCIETY.

In retrospect, it can be said that C. Loomis Allen did very well in planning his route. The Utica trip covered every major interurban center on the interurban network that permitted passage of a conventional interurban car. At one point or another, the Utica trip covered, crossed or connected with virtually every important interurban line that was part of the network. Any increased mileage would have added very little to the overall impact of the trip. Hence, there are grounds for suggesting that the Utica trip covered the interurban network to the maximum practical extent and would have been difficult to beat.

Other Long Trips and Charters

Several other long trips and charters by interurban and electric railway have been recorded through the years. What made the Utica trip unique was its insistence on continuous use of electric power. Although several other long distance trips by interurban are documented, virtually all elected to use steam railroads for a portion of the trip. From the standpoint of records set, the Utica trip excelled substantially in the number of continuous miles travelled by electric power. The following are some of the more noteworthy interurban trips which have been documented.

• What appears to be the first attempt at making the proverbial trip from New York to Chicago by electric line took place in the summer of 1909. J.S. Moulton, the assistant attorney of the Interborough Rapid Transit Company in New York, made the trip to Chicago using regularly scheduled service. The entire trip took nearly four days but included overnight stops. The total fare was $19.67. The total distance was 1,143 miles, 956 miles on electric cars and 187 miles on steam roads.

Although only a year prior to the Utica tour, several segments had to be made on steam trains or alternate routes because various electric lines had not yet been completed.

Moulton used steam railroads from New York City to Hudson and again from Amsterdam to Little Falls. The segment between Syracuse and Rochester included a jog to Auburn since the direct line of the Rochester, Syracuse & Eastern had not yet been completed. Getting across Rochester to the Buffalo, Lockport & Rochester required a streetcar and a short walk because the crossing at Otis Station was yet to be installed. A steam train was used between Wabash and Warsaw, Indiana, because the Winona Interurban had yet to complete its missing link. Finally, a steam suburban train of the Illinois Central was used to get from the Chicago, Lake Shore & South Bend Railway at Pullman (later called Kensington) into downtown Chicago.

• The second known attempt at long distance travel by interurban was not well documented. Mr. A.J. Littlejohn, who was associated with the Beebe Syndicate of New York, made a trip using interurban railways in February of 1910. He started from Oneonta, New York and planned to travel by electric railway to Utica, Syracuse, Buffalo, Cleveland, Chicago and St. Louis. The round trip distance was given as 2,728 miles. It was reported that Mr. Littlejohn reached Conneaut, Ohio on February 5 and arrived in Chicago shortly thereafter. One account indicates that Littlejohn reached Chicago from Oneonta after 1,068 miles of travel in 40 hours of actual traveling time. Presumably, Littlejohn used the recently-completed Winona interurban in order to ride an all-electric route from Oneonta to the outskirts of Chicago.

Unfortunately, no confirmation could be discovered on whether Littlejohn reached St. Louis or made the return trip to Oneonta. However, he would have been forced to ride behind a steam locomotive when entering Chicago. A steam train would also have been necessary between the Chicago-area interurbans and the Illinois Traction System. Hence, the longest all-electric portion of Littlejohn's trip would have been barely over 1,000 miles from Oneonta to the outskirts of Chicago.

• In 1910, Mr. E.C. Van Valkenburgh made a trip from Chicago to New York using interurban lines. It is believed that the trip was taken for the purpose of determining the practicality of tourist and vacation travel by electric railway since the trip was documented in a 1½-page article in *Electric Railway Journal.*

Mr. Van Valkenburgh took nearly a month for the entire trip. He used electric lines where possible, but used steam railroads where no interurban lines were available and also rode a boat for 114 miles. Included were over 800 miles of side trips and excursions. A total of 1,704 miles were covered on electric cars (though steam railroad and boat trips were interspersed). The direct route from Chicago to New York, if electric lines were used whenever possible (which meant via Peru and Fort Wayne[2]), was 1,163 miles at a cost of $19.64. He indicated that this trip could probably be made in 45 to 50 hours of continuous travel.

Van Valkenburgh said that advance planning was difficult (combining Midwest interurban schedules into a single publication had not yet been attempted). However, once underway, he found it easy to get information for the next couple hundred miles. He mentioned that most connections were close or required a wait of not more than 30 minutes. One of his biggest complaints was the lack of uniform baggage regulations on the lines. Van Valkenburgh indicated that interurban fares averaged about 1¾ cents per mile. He said: "When compared with through fares on the steam roads, there is little if any advantage in favor of the electric railway."

• If either Moulton or Van Valkenburgh had chosen the summer of 1918 for their New York-Chicago trek, they could have travelled from New York City to Schenectady, New York, entirely by electric railway except for 27 miles of steam railroad near Troy, New York. This route through New Haven, Connecticut; Springfield, Massachusetts; Pittsfield, Massachusetts; Bennington, Vermont and Hoosick Falls, New York, was possible only during the summer and fall of 1917 and the summer of 1918, the years a 25-mile connecting link of Berkshire Street Railway was in operation. Thus, 236 miles of electric railway travel was added to the New York-Chicago journey.[3]

• An interesting, though non-commercial trip, was made by an Illinois Traction car from St. Louis, Missouri to Sandusky, Ohio in August of 1911. Officials of Illinois Traction made this trip to attend the Cedar Point meeting of the Central Electric Railway

After the abandonment of the Oneida Line, car 502 was assigned to the Wolf Street Shops in Syracuse. Here, for the next seven years, it was used to pull coal cars from the New York Central track to the shop. This photo was taken on August 18, 1938. M.D. McCARTER COLLECTION.

After car 502 was slated for scrapping, the railroad hobbiests made a special effort to obtain a "last formal portrait" in November of 1938. For this occasion the car was specially dressed up with marker lights, a destination sign and a headlight. J.R. McFARLANE COLLECTION.

Association. Several guests from other electric lines were carried along on portions of the trip.

Car 233 of the Illinois Traction System was used. It was the office car of H.E. Chubbuck, general manager of ITS, and contained an office, kitchen, observation room and Pullman-sized berths for six people. The trip started on August 19 and used Illinois Traction trackage from St. Louis to Danville. Since there was no electric link at this point (and never would be), car 233 was towed behind a Big Four steam train the 52 miles from Danville, Illinois to New Ross, Indiana. This section was the only stretch of the trip where the car could not operate under its own power. From New Ross, the car followed interurban lines to Indianapolis, Peru, Fort Wayne, Lima, Findlay, Fostoria, Fremont and Sandusky.

The return was made via Cleveland, Seville, Marion, Columbus, Springfield, Lima, Fort Wayne, Muncie, Indianapolis and back to New Ross. Again, the car had to be hauled by a steam train between New Ross and Danville. From Danville, car 233 followed the Illinois Traction System to Peoria.

The total distance on electric railways was 1,519.2 miles (the car had an odometer) and the average speed was 26.44 miles per hour. The only difficulty encountered was at New Ross on the eastbound trip. The steam train dropped the car on the station siding, about 200 feet from the nearest trolley wire on the Ben Hur Route. A jumper cable had to be used to move the stranded car.

• One of the most interesting examples of an interurban charter was a May, 1916, movement of a three-car Chicago & Milwaukee Electric Railroad train for the members of a Masonic organization. This charter operated a round trip from Milwaukee, Wisconsin to Rockford, Illinois via Chicago over six different lines. Included were the Chicago & Milwaukee Electric, the Northwestern Elevated Railroad Company, the Metropolitan West Side Elevated Railroad Company, the Aurora, Elgin & Chicago Railroad, the Elgin & Belvidere Electric Company, and the Rockford & Interurban Railway. However, the one-way distance was only 177 miles and required less than seven hours of travel. What made this trip particularly unusual is that three chartered cars were operated in multiple unit and they drew power from a third rail while on the two rapid transit lines and while on the Aurora, Elgin & Chicago. It might be noted that at the time of this charter the C&ME (eventually called the North Shore Line) had not yet started regular operation of passenger trains into downtown Chicago over the elevated tracks.

• In the autumn of 1923, Mr. Fred Tedrahn attempted to make a trip from Evanston, Illinois to New York City via electric traction. He reached a dead end at Conneaut, Ohio because the Cleveland & Erie line had already been abandoned. Tedrahn boarded a steam train to Erie and returned to using interurbans at that point.

• What was probably the last of the great interurban tours took place in June of 1937 when Frank Donovan Jr. made a trip from Cleveland, Ohio to St. Louis, Missouri using interurban lines wherever possible. Regularly scheduled trains were used for the entire trip. One portion of the trip had to be changed because of a recent abandonment, one segment of the trip was only months from abandonment and all of the Ohio and Indiana trackage used would last no more than four more years.

Expectedly, Donovan rode the Lake Shore Electric from Cleveland to Toledo, but used the local line via Norwalk. At Toledo, he boarded the *Daniel Boone* on the Cincinnati & Lake Erie Railroad which was operated with a single lightweight, high speed car. The trackage between Toledo and Lima would only last five more months and would be abandoned in November (thus separating northern Ohio and southern Ohio interurban lines for the first time since 1905). Donovan's original itinerary called for him to go west from Dayton to Indianapolis (the last link between the Ohio and Indiana interurban lines) but this had just been abandoned on May 9. Hence, he decided to continue south on the Cincinnati & Lake Erie to Cincinnati. Here, a steam train on the L&N was used to reach Louisville.

Donovan then went north on the Indiana Railroad from Louisville to Indianapolis, Peru and Fort Wayne, effectively retracing the route of car 502 some 27 years earlier. He returned to Indianapolis via the Indiana Railroad line via Muncie and then continued west to Terre Haute. From Terre Haute, Indiana, to Danville, Illinois, Donovan used a steam train on the C&EI. The last interurban used was the Illinois Terminal. St. Louis was reached via Decatur, Bloomington, Mackinaw Junction, and Springfield — a less-than-direct route that permitted Donovan to ride the three main lines of the IT.

Donovan's tour covered 1,277 miles in seven days. Of this, 1,113 miles were by trolley at a cost of $19.64 and 164 miles by steam train for $3.05. Actual travel time on the 14 electric cars and trains used was only 38½ hours.

• It might be noted that special cars were regularly operated to meetings of the Central Electric Railway Association over the years, including at least one movement over Oneida Railway. In addition, there were many equipment moves where cars were shuttled to a new buyer under their own power on a long and interesting route. Like the Illinois Traction movement mentioned above, many of these are very interesting but do not reflect substantially on the accomplishment of the Uticans since these were not commercial trips with passengers.

Car 502

In many respects, car 502 was the star of the 1910 Utica charter. Surviving records indicate that the car operated flawlessly over the numerous interurban and streetcar lines. Faith in car 502 was apparently justified since the car was undoubtedly the most prominent and one of the longest surviving pieces of equipment of the Oneida Railway.

Oneida Railway opened service between Utica and Syracuse on June 16, 1907. Car 502, brand new at that time, headed a first special passenger train to Syracuse for officials and dignitaries on June 15. Whether for this reason or another, car 502 was selected by C. Loomis Allen for the May, 1910 charter trip.

After May of 1910, car 502 lost its special interior and lettering and returned to the more mundane task of running scheduled service on the Oneida Railway between Utica and Syracuse. In the early 1920s, car 502

By the late 1930s, car 502 was just another old interurban car assigned to a mundane task at Wolf Street Shops. However, when the order came to scrap the car, the railroad historians remembered its significance. As a result, George L. Barrett made a special trip to photograph the passing of car 502 on the day of scrapping. These three photos were eventually passed on to Charles L. Ballard and were printed for this book by the Oneida County Historical Society. Above is the final interior photo of the car. Although far from clean, the car retained its seats and most of its fixtures until the end. BARRETT/BALLARD/ONEIDA COUNTY HISTORICAL SOCIETY.

This is the final exterior photo of car 502. It was taken by George L. Barrett just prior to the car being burned and scrapped. BARRETT/BALLARD/ONEIDA COUNTY HISTORICAL SOCIETY.

The final photo of the three shows car 502 immediately after it was burned at Wolf Street Shops. Both trucks and the bottom of the car remain in evidence. In the background are some local streetcars which would meet a similar fate. BARRETT/BALLARD/ONEIDA COUNTY HISTORICAL SOCIETY.

and similar cars on the Oneida Line of New York State Railway, were substantially overhauled. They emerged with steel sheathing and were equipped for double end operation. At this time the end train doors were removed and replaced by solid ends without train doors.

By the late 1920s, the Oneida Line of New York State Railways had lost most of its passengers to the private automobile. Only a single car was necessary to handle the hourly service between Utica and Syracuse and multiple unit trains ran only during the rush hours. Abandonment of the line finally came on December 31, 1930.

Following abandonment, cars 500, 502 and four other cars were sent to Syracuse for disposition. All other cars remained in Utica and were presumably scrapped. Car 502 was once again selected for special duty. This time it was sent to the Wolf Street Shops in Syracuse. For at least seven years, car 502 was used to pull coal cars from the New York Central Railroad to the shops. Reports indicate that the car was finally scrapped in late 1938. As such, it survived nearly all of the lines it had operated over and cars it had encountered on the famous charter trip in May of 1910.

Car 502 is shown on the transfer table at Wolf Street yard in an earlier and happier age. The photo was probably taken in the early 1920s while the car was being overhauled because the trolley poles indicate the car was still set up for single end operation while the steel sheathing has already been applied. ONEIDA COUNTY HISTORICAL SOCIETY.

The Longest Interurban Charter • 85

DISBURSEMENTS

Mohawk Engraving Co.,	$ 13.00
H. E. Lovett,——Mat,	2.50
J. B. Carroll,——Buttons,	41.65
W. T. Witherall & Co.,——Syphons, etc.,	5.50
Williams & Morgan,	13.50
Miss Alice Howarth,——Stenog. services,	10.00
George Gammell,	6.00
Frank J. Baker,——Florist,	8.00
Sherman & Latcher,——Canes,	22.50
W. D. Jones & Son,——Printing,	40.25
J. M. Jones & Co.,——Lines,	1.65
Bagg's Hotel,	43.50
Bowen & Perry,——Insurance,	63.00
Flags at Syracuse,	.75
George F. Murray,——Cigars,	15.15
T. W. Johnson for William,	50.00
M. J. Brayton,——Present,	40.00
Pilot of car Syracuse to Rochester,	3.00
Water,——Louisville,	2.20
Water,——Indianapolis,	7.50
Dinners,——Fremont,—Ohio,	4.00
Postage,	.50
Magazines,	.60
Maher Bros.,——Suit of clothes for William,	23.50
J. B. Wells, Son & Co.,——Carpet and Chairs,	241.30
Bowen & Perry,——Insurance for Crew,	6.00
Roberts Hardware Co.,——Refrigerator, etc.,	45.33
Mathews & Co.,——Typewriter,	3.00
T. W. Johnson for William,	25.00
Miss Alice Howarth,——Stenog. services,	10.00
Utica Chamber of Commerce,——Postage,	12.20

HOTELS

Hotel Seneca,——Rochester,	56.10
Hotel Lafayette, Luncheon——Buffalo,	18.75
Reed House,——Erie,	33.00
Reed House,——Erie, Baggage,	3.00
The Hollenden, Cleveland,—2 Days & Lunches, Baggage,——Going and coming,	145.25
Hotel Chittenden,——Columbus, Ohio,	69.00
Hotel Chittenden,——Columbus, Ohio, Baggage,	2.00
Hotel Algonquin, Dayton—Ohio,	90.00
Hotel Algonquin, Dayton—Ohio, Baggage,	2.50
Hotel Claypool, Indianapolis,	58.58
Hotel Claypool, Indianapolis, Baggage,	2.00
Hotel Seelbach, Louisville,	55.00
Hotel Seelbach, Louisville, Baggage,	3.00
Hotel Claypool, Indianapolis,	56.45
Hotel Claypool, Indianapolis, Baggage,	2.00
Hotel Anthony, Fort Wayne,	47.00
Hotel Anthony, Fort Wayne, Baggage,	2.00
	$1406.71

FINAL REPORT OF THE TREASURER OF THE TROLLEY TOUR

RECEIPTS

22 Members at $110.00 each,	$2420.00
Contributed from M. J. Brayton,	50.00
Receipts from Banquet,	3.75
Bennett for room,	2.50
Incidentals,	9.12
Mr. Batsford, For refrigerator,	10.00
Oneida Railway Co., Advertising,	33.60
Total,	**$2528.97**

	Disbursements	Receipts
Amount Forwarded	$1406.71	$2528.97
Hotel Secor, Toledo,	57.00	
Hotel Secor, Toledo, Baggage,	2.00	
Hotel Pontchartrain, Detroit,	68.40	
Hotel Pontchartrain, Detroit, Baggage,	2.00	
Hotel Lafayette, Buffalo,	44.00	
Hotel Lafayette, Buffalo, Baggage,	2.00	

TRANSPORTATION

Columbus, Marion & Bucyrus Railway,	5.40	
New York State Railways,	4.00	
New York State Railways,	4.00	
Ohio Railway Electric Co.,	161.25	
Sandusky, Norwalk & Mansfield Railway,	9.00	
Indianapolis & Louisville Traction,	47.00	
Louisville & Northern Lighting Co.,	11.25	
Indiana Union Traction Co.,	25.00	
International Railway Co.,	10.50	
Oneida Railway Co.,	421.49	
Total,	**$2281.00**	
		$2281.00
Balance,		$ 247.97
Dividend, 10%,		$ 220.00
Final Balance,		**$ 27.97**

The Utica Electric Railway Tour was financed through a special fund which was administered by F.W. Bensberg as treasurer for the group. Most of the fund was created by contributions of $110 by each of 22 passengers. A copy of the final financial report survives as a typewritten carbon copy in the Utica scrapbook. The quality of the original is too poor to permit reproduction but the basic data has been duplicated on these two pages.

Several of the entries are as yet unexplained. The dividend may have gone back to the passengers, thereby reducing their fare to $100 each. It might be noted that most of the interurban lines failed to charge for transportation and storage. The highest fee went to the Ohio Electric Railway, most likely because the trolley pilgrims used three different segments of this company's trackage. The next highest fee went to the Indianapolis & Louisville Traction Company which undoubtedly reflects the need for hauling car 502 over this company's tracks. The charge from Oneida Railway Co. undoubtedly represents the charter fee for car 502 since track charges appear to be listed under New York State Railways. For some unexplained reason, the charge for the pilot from Syracuse to Rochester appears on the previous page instead of under transportation.

The entry for the typewriter has never been explained but may have been for the on-board reporters to type out their material. It would have been interesting to know what type of refrigerator was used but it is noted that it was sold to Mr. Batsford after the trip.

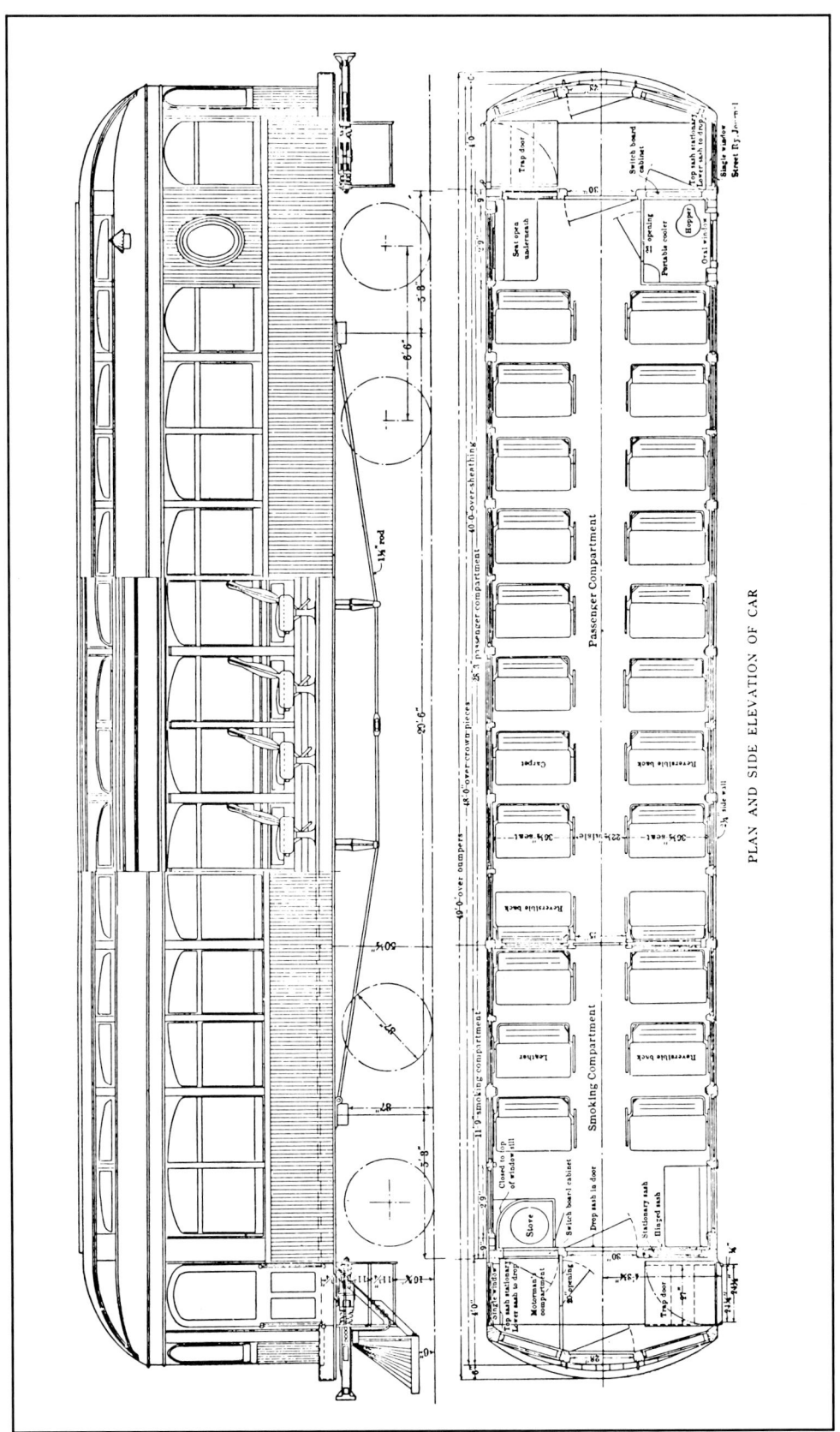

Car plan and side elevation for cars 500-528 of the Oneida Railway Company. These cars were built by the J.G. Brill Company of Philadelphia in 1907 and started service on the Oneida Railway. This reflects the original appearance and arrangement for car 502 prior to the modifications for the 1910 trip. The diagram is reprinted from *The New York State Railways.* SHELDEN S. KING.

Epilogue

It Was A Remarkable Trip

At some future time, when the electric roads of this country shall have been further extended and connected under a smaller number of managements, someone will write a history of electric traction development in this country. He will then tell of the "first long trip" in one trolley car — that of the Utica business men who returned last evening — and it will become an historical event. Magazine articles already have appeared describing the trips of one man from one distant point to another by trolley, making changes and often long jumps to connect the scattered lines. But the Utica trip is the first long continuous trip by electric traction on this continent, and probably is as long as could be taken in any country in the world. It was not 2,000 miles long straightaway, of course, but it extended through great sections of six States, and it was a triumph in planning and in detail. The scheme originated with C. Loomis Allen, General Manager of the New York state line of electric traction, and its happy conclusion last evening should give Mr. Allen no small degree of satisfaction.

Utica in its history has had many "firsts." It has added another to the list; and in so doing it has incidentally given herself new and additional prominence. To those who entered with Mr. Allen so heartily into the project and have sustained the good name, fame and importance of the city in other places during this pioneer journey of an electric coach, the city may well extend its thanks and give a hearty welcome home.

Utica Observer
May 24, 1910

Notes

Acknowledgements

1. **Books:** *Buffalo & Lake Erie Traction Co.*, (Gordon), p. 3 — *The Electric Interurban Railways in America*, (Hilton and Due), p. 42 — *Here Comes The Trolley!*, (Gurley), p. 28 — *The Interurban Era*, (Middleton), p. 44-45 — *The Interurban Lines of Central and Western New York State*, CERA Bulletin 44, (McFarlane), p. 31-32 — *The New York State Railways*, (King), p. 83-85 — *Rochester, Lockport and Buffalo R.R.*, (Gordon), p. 6-7 — *Traction Classics*, Vol. 1, (Middleton), p. 40-41.
Periodicals: "2000 Miles by Trolley," *Railroad Magazine*, April, 1961 (Middleton), p. 18-19 — *NOT&L News*, May-June, 1950, (Weaver).

Chapter One

1. News clipping from the *Scrapbook Of The 1910 Utica Electric Railway Tour* at the Oneida County Historical Society.

Chapter Two

1. The actual list of the Utica businessmen on the trip is still not totally clear. It is known that 22 individuals paid for a seat on the tour but research has only been able to confirm these 21 listed individuals as having actually ridden the trip. At this time it is not known whether that last seat was paid for by another businessman or by C. Loomis Allen to cover himself or either of his two railway superintendents (T.C. Cherry and E.J. Wright) while on trip duty. Lists of passengers were made or published at several locations including Utica, Dayton, Louisville and Toledo. All of the individuals shown appear on all four lists noted with the following exceptions: Barnard and Hind are missing from the Louisville list but are shown on the other three lists. Both are also mentioned elsewhere in the accounts of the trip. Bensberg and Schachtel are missing from the Toledo list but appear on the other other three lists. The participation of both gentlemen is not questioned since Bensberg is mentioned four times in accounts of the trip other than the lists of participants, and Schachtel was the on-board reporter responsible for most of the Utica news articles. Williams is missing from the Utica and Louisville lists but appears in the Dayton and Toledo lists. It is interesting that one listing of passengers in Dayton provides nine names that do not appear elsewhere — possibly friends or others on the car that wanted to get their names in print. The name of F.V. Benkley, capitalist, also appears in the Toledo list.

Chapter Three

1. The Utica scrapbook clearly states that Arthur Hind did not board the car in Utica but was picked up at Clark Mills, the location of his large plush factory. However, one of the individuals in the South Utica photo of car 502 was identified as Arthur Hind in a 1949 caption. These two items are contradictory and no answer has yet been uncovered.
2. There was a steam railroad crossing at grade in Syracuse but this was on trackage owned by the Syracuse, Lake Shore & Northern and not on the Rochester, Syracuse & Eastern.
3. Although the interurban network is generally said to have extended from Elkhart Lake, Wisconsin to Little Falls (or Oneonta), New York, there never was a direct interurban track link at Chicago. Interurban passengers arriving in Chicago from the east on the Chicago Lake Shore & South Bend (later the South Shore Line) were carried into Chicago by steam powered trains of the Illinois Central in the early years. At all times passengers were required to walk or take public transportation a short distance to board a North Shore Line or Aurora Elgin & Chicago train. Connections to the Kankakee line or the Chicago & Joliet required an intermediate ride on an "L" or streetcar. There never was a direct or practical method to move a car under electric power from the Chicago Lake Shore & South Bend to the other Chicago interurbans.
4. The Central Electric Railway Association was a trade association of the interurban industry that, among other things, sought to promote the interline ticketing of passengers and cooperative freight operations as well as compatibility of equipment. Whysall's regular occupation was president of the Columbus, Marion & Bucyrus Railroad.
5. Harding remained in politics. In 1914 he was elected to the U.S. Senate. Harding was nominated for the presidency in 1920 and was subsequently elected to become the 29th president of the United States.
6. The several accounts of the arrival at Dayton show different times. 9:50 a.m. appears to be the correct time.
7. Oddly enough, both accounts published in Dayton newspapers list C. Loomis Allen with the group and not T.C. Cherry. However, reports filed from on board the car clearly state that Allen left the group on May 13 and did not return until the evening of May 17.
8. "New Yorkers Seeking To Learn Success Of Middle West Cities." *Dayton Journal,* May 15, 1910, p. 7A.
9. Two years later, the three interurban lines between Indianapolis and Louisville would be combined by Sam Insull into the 117-mile Interstate Public Service Company. In 1931, they would become part of the Indiana Railroad. Overhead wire voltage between Indianapolis and Louisville was standarized in the early 1920s.

PRECEDING PAGE

An eastbound Cleveland, Southwestern & Columbus interurban car approaches a crossing with the Lake Shore & Michigan Southern on Rte. 61 on the east side of Norwalk, Ohio. The photo dates to about 1910, the year that car 502 used this same crossing. Both railroads have since been abandoned and the crossing has been gone for decades. DAVID SCHAFER COLLECTION.

Chapter Three (continued)

10. The private car was probably the "Lawton," which was the company private car used as an office or business car.

Chapter Four

1. "Champion Traction Tourists Are Entertained In Dayton." *Dayton Daily News,* May 14, 1910, p. 13.
2. There never was a direct electric railway link between Toledo, Ohio, and South Bend, Indiana. Hence, passengers wishing to take electric railways between Toledo and Chicago had to detour south via Lima, Fort Wayne and Peru.

Chapter Four (continued)

3. **First Day**   **Miles**
   New York (City Hall)-New Haven, Conn. 92
   New Haven-Springfield, Mass. 68
   Second Day
   Springfield-Pittsfield, Mass. 57
   Pittsfield-Bennington, VT 40
   Bennington-Hoosick Falls, NY 15
   Hoosick Falls-Troy, NY (Boston & Maine - Steam) *27
   Troy Union Station-Schenectady, NY 17
   Total Electric Railway Mileage **289**
   Less portion of Van Valkenburgh's trip obviated by use of above route:
   New York City-Hudson, NY (Hudson River Steamer) . .*114
   Hudson-Albany, NY 37
   Albany-Schenectady, NY 16
   Total Electric Railway Mileage **53**
   Net Additional Electric Railway Miles **236**
   * — *Non-electric mileage, not included in totals*

LUNCHEON FOR THE

"UTICA BOOSTERS"

GIVEN BY THE

DETROIT BOARD OF COMMERCE

FRIDAY, MAY 20, 1910

BELLE ISLE CASINO

Menu
                                Martini Cocktail

Consomme

Olives   Radishes

Planked Whitefish

        Squab   **Burgundy**

New Asparagus   Green Peas

Cream Potatoes

Combination Salad

Ice Cream   Cake

Crackers   Cheese

Coffee
                            Cigars

Souvenir menu printed for the luncheon on Friday, May 20, 1910 at the Belle Isle Casino in Detroit. The Detroit Board of Commerce sponsored the luncheon as a reception to honor the Utica trolley pilgrims upon their arrival in Detroit. ONEIDA COUNTY HISTORICAL SOCIETY.

Bibliography

Books

Campbell, George V. *Days Of The North Shore Line.* Delavan, Wis.: National Bus Trader, 1985.

Christiansen, Harry. *Lake Shore Electric.* Cleveland, Ohio: Harry Christiansen, 1963.

----------. *New Lake Shore Electric.* Lakewood, Ohio: Trolley Lore, 1978.

----------. *New Northern Ohio's Interurbans and Rapid Transit Railways.* Euclid, Ohio: Trolley Lore, 1983.

----------. *Ohio Trolley Trails,* Volume 1. Euclid, Ohio: Western Reserve Historical Society, 1971.

----------. *Trolley Trails Through Greater Cleveland And Northern Ohio.* Lakewood, Ohio: Western Reserve Historical Society, 1975.

Electric Railways of Indiana, Bulletin 101 of the Central Electric Railfans' Association. Chicago: 1957.

Electric Railways of Indiana, Bulletin 102 of the Central Electric Railfans' Association. Chicago: 1958.

Electric Railways of Indiana, Bulletin 104 of the Central Electric Railfans' Association. Chicago: 1960.

Electric Railways of Michigan, Bulletin 103 of the Central Electric Railfans' Association. Chicago: 1959.

Electric Railways of Northeastern Ohio, Bulletin 108 of the Central Electric Railfans' Association. Chicago: 1965.

Gordon, William R. *Buffalo & Lake Erie Traction Co.* Rochester, N.Y.: William Reed Gordon, 1977.

----------. *Rochester, Lockport And Buffalo R.R.* Rochester, N.Y.: William Reed Gordon, 1963.

----------. *90 Years of Buffalo Railways.* Rochester, N.Y.: William Reed Gordon, 1970.

Gordon, William R. and McFarlane, James R. *The Rochester, Syracuse & Eastern.* Rochester, N.Y.: William Reed Gordon, 1961.

Gurley, Robert G. *Here Comes The Trolley!* Traction Press, 1964.

Hague, Wilbur E., and Hise, Kirk F. *The Detroit, Monroe & Toledo Short Line Railway.* Forty Fort, Pa.: Harold E. Cox, 1986.

Hardin, Richard. *Louisville & Interurban Railroad,* Bulletin 90 of the Central Electric Railfans' Association. Chicago: 1950.

Hilton, George W. and Due, John F. *The Electric Interurban Railways in America.* Stanford, Calif.: Stanford University Press, 1960.

Johnson, James D. *The Lincoln Land Traction.* Wheaton, Ill.: The Traction Orange Co., 1965.

Keenan, Jack. *Cincinnati & Lake Erie Railroad.* San Marino, Calif.: Golden West Books, 1974.

King, Shelden S. *The New York State Railways.* Elmira Heights, N.Y.: Shelden S. King, 1970.

McFarlane, J.R. *The Interurban Lines of Central and Western New York State,* Bulletin 44 of the Central Electric Railfans' Association. Chicago: 1943.

Middleton, William D. *The Interurban Era.* Milwaukee, Wis.: Kalmbach Publishing Co., 1961.

----------. *Traction Classics — The Interurbans, The Great Wood and Steel Cars,* V. 1. San Marino, Calif.: Golden West Books, 1983.

Nestle, David F. *The Leatherstocking Route — From the Mohawk to the Susquehanna by Interurban.* David F. Nestle, 1959.

Terre Haute, Indianapolis & Eastern Traction Company, Bulletin 30 of the Central Electric Railfans' Association. Chicago: 1941.

Timetables of Electric Railways of Indiana, Ohio, Kentucky, Michigan, Bulletin 59 of the Central Electric Railfans' Association. Chicago: 1945.

Periodicals

"2000 Mile Trolley Tour," *ERA Headlights,* Vol. 3, No. 6 (June 15, 1941),6.

Donovan, Frank Jr. "A Thousand Miles By Trolley," *Railroad Magazine,* December, 1937,116-125.

"Long Journey Of Illinois Traction Office Car," *Electric Railway Journal,* Vol. 38, No. 10 (September 2, 1911), 395-396.

"Long Trip By Trolley," *Electric Railway Journal,* Vol. 35, No. 11 (March 12, 1910),461.

Middleton, William D. "2,000 Miles By Trolley," *Railroad Magazine,* Vol. 72, No. 3 (April, 1961),18-19.

Moulton, J.S. "New York To Chicago By Electric Railway," *Electric Railway Journal,* Vol. 34, No. 9 (August 28, 1909),321-322.

Periodicals (continued)

Plachno, Larry. "The Longest Electric Railway Charter," *The Journal of Erie Studies*, Vol. 17, No. 1 (Spring, 1988), 27-39.

"Progress Of Utica Trolley Tour," *Electric Railway Journal*, Vol. 35, No. 21 (May 21, 1910), 908.

"Proposed Trip From Utica To Indianapolis," *Electric Railway Journal*, Vol. 35, No. 10 (March 5, 1910), 426.

"Successful Completion Of The Utica Electric Railway Trip," *Electric Railway Journal*, Vol. 35, No. 22 (May 28, 1910), 950.

"The Utica Trolley Trip," *Electric Railway Journal*, Vol. 35, No. 22 (May 28, 1910), 931.

Van Valkenburgh, E.C. "From Chicago to New York On Electric Cars," *Electric Railway Journal*, Vol. 36, No. 13 (September 24, 1910), 470-471.

Weaver, Dudley. *NOT&L News*, May-June, 1950.

Newspapers

"A Jolly Good Set Of Fellows," *Marion Daily Mirror*, 14 May 1910.

"Champion Traction Tourists Are Entertained In Dayton," *Dayton Daily News*, 14 May 1910, 13.

"First Great Trolley Trip Came To Happy Close," *Utica Observer*, 24 May 1910.

"In Cleveland: The Sewage Cocktail Was 'Discovered'," *Utica Observer-Dispatch*, 8 May 1949, 12A.

"Longest Trolley Trip Started To-Day," *Utica Observer*, 10 May 1910.

"Men From Utica Come Today," *Kokomo Dispatch*, 18 May 1910, 4.

"Men From Utica Soon Due Here," *Kokomo Dispatch*, 17 May 1910, 1.

"New Yorkers Seeking To Learn Success Of Middle West Cities," *Dayton Journal*, 15 May 1910, 7A.

"Seeing How Things Are Done In Other Cities With A View To Bettering Utica," *Norwalk Daily Reflector*, 13 May 1910, 1.

"Special Trolley Carrying Utica Business Men," *Erie Daily Times*, 12 May 1910, 1.

Newspapers (continued)

"Take 2,000-Mile Ride On Trolley," *The Cleveland Leader*, 13 May 1910.

"Trolley Tourists Are Nearing Home," *Utica Observer*, 23 May 1910.

"Trolley Trip Spread Utica's Fame," *Utica Observer-Dispatch*, 1 May 1949, 1.

"Utica Boomers," *Fremont Daily News*, 21 May 1910, 3.

"Utica Business Men," *Norwalk Evening Herald*, 13 May, 1910.

"Utica Business Men On Search For Ideas," *Ohio State Journal* [Columbus], 14 May 1910, 7.

"Utica Business Men Return Home," *Erie Daily Times*, 24 May 1910, 8.

"Utica Business Men Will Be Here," *Erie Daily Times*, 10 May 1910, 2.

"Utica Merchants Visit Marion," *Marion Daily Mirror*, 13 May 1910.

"Utica Party Come And Gone," *Erie Daily Times*, 12 May 1910, 1.

"Utica Trolley Car Party Left City 31 Years Ago For 2,000-Mile Tour," *Utica Observer-Dispatch*, 10 May 1941.

"Want Toledo Ideas," *Toledo Daily Blade*, 20 May 1910.

Other References

Marlette, Jerry. *Interstate (The story of rail operations of Interstate Public Service)*. Unpublished manuscript, due for publication by Transportation Trails in 1988.

McFarlane, J.R. "Utica Electric Railway Tour, May 10-23, 1910." Unpublished manuscript.

Plachno, Larry. "The Perfect Interurban Trip." Unpublished manuscript, due for publication by *Traction & Trolleys Quarterly* in late 1988.

Scrapbook Of The 1910 Utica Electric Railway Tour. Assembled 1910 from news clippings and souvenirs of the trip. Collection of Oneida County Historical Society, Utica, New York.

Warrick, Bill and McLellan, David. *The Lake Shore & Michigan Southern Railway*. Unpublished manuscript, due for publication by Transportation Trails in 1988.

An interurban car of the Sandusky, Norwalk & Mansfield Electric Railway poses in front of the company's elaborate depot in North Fairfield, Ohio. Car 502 passed this same location. The photo was taken prior to 1910. DAVID SCHAFER COLLECTION.

Index

Page numbers shown in *italics* indicate primary subject or location of photographs.

— A —
Agne, Jacob*, 25, 35, *51*
Akins, A.E., 45
Akron, Ohio, 79
Albion, NY., 37
Alfred University, 28, 29
Allen & Peck, Inc., 29
Allen, C. Loomis*, 9, 19, 20, 21, 23, 24, 25, 27, *28*, 29, 31, 33, 35, 37, 45, 51, 59, 61, 63, 67, 69, 71, 73, 75, 77, 78, 79, 81, 83
Allen, Henry C., 28
Allen, W. Fred*, 25, *50, 51*
Amsterdam, NY., 81
Andrews, Horace L., 28, 29
Andrews-Stanley Syndicate, 28, 29
Anthony, L.L., 61
Ashtabula, Ohio, 20, 41, 43, 69, 77 Harbor, *42*
Atwood, W.B., 41, 43
Auburn & Northern, 35
Auburn & Syracuse, 25, 35
Auburn, NY., 19, 20, 35, 81
Aurora, Elgin & Chicago Railroad, 83
Austin, Ind., *54*

— B —
Bagg's Hotel, *10*, 11, 23, 25, 31, 71, 73
Baker, Frank (Fred) J.*, 25, 27, 31, 39, 41, *50*
Baker, William T., 19
Barnard, Charles E.*, 25, *43, 51*, 53
Batsford, Edwin T.*, 25, *50*, 87
Battle Creek, Mich., 79
Beach, D.F., 71
Beatty, H.C., 35, 37
Becker, J., 27
Beebe Syndicate, 25, 29, 35, 81
Bennington, Vt., 81
Bensberg, F.W.*, 19, 25, 27, 41, *43, 51*, 87
Berkshire Street Railway, 81
Berlin Heights, Ohio, *8*
Big Four Railroad, *Louisville Bridge*, 55, 57, *58*
Birmingham, Ohio, *46*
Bloomington, Ill., 83
Bonn, John, 71
Brady, Arthur, 61
Brill Company, J.G., 22, 23, 66, 69, 88
Brockport, NY., *36*, 37
Brock, William L.*, 25
Brocton, NY., 39
Brush, George M., 69
Brush, Matthew C., 39, 69
Bucyrus, Ohio, 45, 47, 49
Buffalo & Lackawanna Traction Co., 39, 75
Buffalo & Lake Erie Traction Company, 19, *36, 38*, 39, 69, *70*, 71, 75
Buffalo, Lockport & Rochester Railway, 15, 19, 25, 27, 29, 35, *36*, 37, *70*, 71, 81
Buffalo, NY., 19, 20, 37, 39, 41, 67, 71, 81
Burkhardt, F.A., 63
Butterfield, John, 9

— C —
Cain, J.H., 37, 71
Calish, Julius C., 39, 71
Campbell, J.M., 37, 71
Canastota, NY., 33, *72*
Canton, Ohio, 79
Cassidy, Fred A.*, 25, *50, 51*, 53
Central Electric Railway Association, 47, 81
Ceylon Junction, Ohio, 69
Cherry, T.C.*, 21, 25, 27, 29, 31, 33, 35, 45
Cherry, Mrs. T.C., 45
Chicago & Milwaukee Electric Railroad, 83
Chicago, Ill., 13, 79, 81, 83
Chicago Junction, Ohio, *46*
Chicago, Lake Shore & South Bend, 79, 81
Chicago, South Bend & Northern Indiana Railway, 61
Chubbuck, H.E., 83
Cincinnati & Lake Erie Railroad, 83
Cincinnati, Ohio, 13, 15, 20, 63 *Proposed side trip*, 23, 31, 51, 77, 79
Clark, Charles H., 43
Clark Mills, NY., 9, 33, *33*
Clark, Theodore W., 28
Clark, Wilbur S.*, 25, *51*
Cleveland & Erie Railway, *40*, 41, *68*, 69, 79, 83
Cleveland, Ohio, 15, 19, 20, 28, 41, 43, 45, 47, 49, 65, 67, 69, 79, 81, 83
Cleveland, Painesville & Ashtabula Railroad, 41, 43, 75
Cleveland, Painesville & Eastern Railroad, 41, *42*, 43, *68*, 69, 75
Cleveland, Southwestern & Columbus Railway, *8, 16, 44*, 45, *46*, 47, *48*, 75, 79, *90*
Cole, F.E., 55
Cole, J. Soley*, 19, 23, 25, 49
Collins, C.C., 65
Columbus, Delaware & Marion Railway, 49, 75
Columbus, Marion & Bucyrus Railway, 19, 47, 49, 75
Columbus, Ohio, 19, 20, 45, 49, 55, 79, 83
Conkling, Roscoe, 9
Conneaut & Erie Traction Company, *see Cleveland & Erie Railway*
Conneaut, Ohio, 41, 69, 81, 83
Conrail, 11
Cook, E.J., 71

— D —
Dallam, Clarence, 57
Danville, Ill., 83
Dayton & Troy, 65
Dayton & Western Traction Co., *52*,53
Dayton, Ohio, 15, 20, 23, 49, 51, *52*, 53, 63, 65, 77, 79, 83
Dean, D.W., 69
Decatur, Ill., 83
Delaware, Lackawanna & Western Railroad, 9, 11
Delaware, Ohio, 49
Delaware Otsego Railroad System, 11
Detroit, Mich., 15, 20, 25, 67, 79 Detroit, Monroe & Toledo Short Line Ry., *66*, 67

Detroit United Lines, 66, 67
Donovan, Frank Jr., 83
Douglas, Dr. E.H., 35

— E —
East Springfield, Pa., 40
Edenburg, Ind., *54*, 55
Elgin & Belvidere Electric Company, 83
Elkhart Lake, Wis., 13
Elyria, Ohio, *44*, 45, 47, 69
Emmons, C.D., 60, 61
Empire State Railroad, 25
Empire United Railways, Inc., 29
Erie, Pa., 19, 20, 39, 41, 69
Espy, J.C., 43
Evanston, Ill., 83
Everett-Moore Syndicate, 67

— F —
Faber, G.E., 45
Fairfield, Ohio, 51
Farnham, NY., *38*, 39, 69, *70*
Findlay, Ohio, 65, 83
Findlay Street Railway, 65
Flint, E.C., 41
Flint, Mich., 79
Foltz, S.A., 47
Fort Wayne & Findlay Railroad, 63
Fort Wayne & Northern Indiana Traction Company, 63
Fort Wayne & Wabash Valley Traction Company, *60*, 61, *62*, 63
Fort Wayne, Ind., 15, 20, 61, 63, 79, 81, 83
Fort Wayne, Van Wert & Lima Traction Company, 6, 63
Fostoria, Ohio, 83
Fox, E.T., 31
Fredonia, NY., 39
Fremont, Ohio, *14*, 20, 65, 67, 69, 78, 83
French, S.H., 25
Fuller, Charles Y.*, 25

— G —
Galion, Ohio, 47, *48*, 61
Goshen, Ind., 13, 17, 37, 61
Gowen, C.R., 21, 31, 71
Grand Rapids, Mich., 79
Grant, General Ulysses S., 9
Guillaume, Dr. Clement T.*, 25, *50*
Gunn Motor, 67

— H —
Hall, John, 71
Harding, Warren G., 49
Harrigan, J.R., 49
Harvie, W.J., 31
Hayes, Rutherford B., 67
Higley, W.T., 71
Hind, Arthur*, 9, 25, 31, 33
Hollenden Hotel, 45, *69*
Hoosick Falls, NY., 81
Hotaling, George, 71
Hotel Utica, 9, 23, 24
Hudson, NY., 81
Huntington, Ind., 62

— I —
Illinois Central, 81
Illinois Traction System, 81, 83
Indiana Railroad, 78, 83

Indiana Union Traction Company, 17, *60*, 61
Indianapolis & Louisville Traction Company, *54*, 55, 59, 87
Indianapolis, Columbus & Eastern, 49, 51
Indianapolis, Columbus & Southern, *54,55*, 59
Indianapolis, Ind., 15, 17, 19, 20, 53, 55, 59, 61, 79, 83
Indianapolis Traction Terminal, *12, 59*
Interborough Rapid Transit Co., 81
International Railway, 15, 37, 71
Interstate Public Service, *58*
Irwin, Joseph I., 55
Irwin, William G., 55

- J -
Jackson, William*, 25, 31, 45, 51
Jeffersonville, Ind., 55
Johnson, D.M.*, 31
Johnson, E., 47
Johnson, Tom W.*, 19, 23, 25, 27, 31, *43, 49, 50, 51, 57*
Johnson, William T., 27
Jordan, Joseph, 41, 43, 69

- K -
Kernan, Francis, 9
Key, John F., 67
Kokomo, Ind., 20, 61, 77
Kokomo, Marion & Western Traction Company, 61

- L -
Lafayette, Ind., 61, 79
Lake Erie & Western Railroad, 69
Lake Shore & Michigan Southern Railway, *14*, 39, 41, *90*
Lake Shore Electric Railway, *4, 14, 15*, 16, 47, 65, *66*, 67, 69, *78*, 83
Lake Shore Junction, 35
Lansing, Mich., 79
Lebanon, Ind., 79
Lehigh Valley Railroad, 6
Lersch, Mrs. John, 45
Lima & Toledo Traction Company, 63
Lima Electric Railway & Light Co., 63
Lima, Ohio, *6*, 20, *63*, 65, 79, 83
Lisle, D.E., 67
Little Falls, NY., 13, 25, 27, 35, 37, 43, 69, 73, 77, 81
Littlejohn, A.J., 81
Lockport, NY., 37
Lorain, Ohio, 69
Lorain Street Railway Company, 28
Louisville & Interurban Railroad, 55
Louisville & Northern Railway & Lighting Company, 55, 59
Louisville, Ky., 13, 19, 15, 20, 55, *56, 57, 58*, 59, 77, 83
Louisville Traction Company, *57*
Love, Henry M.*, 25, 35, 37, 55
Love, Ozro, 37
Lyons, NY., 35, *72*

- M -
Mackinaw Junction, Ill., 83
Maher, John L.*, 25, 38, 39, 41, 43, 50, 51
Mansfield, Ohio, 20, 45, 47, 79
Mansfield Railway Light & Power Company, *47*
Marion, Ohio, 47, 49, 61, 83
Maryland Electric Railways Co., 25, 29
Mather, Thomas H., 28
Maumee Valley Railway & Light Company, 65
McLean, Fred*, 25
Mentor, Ohio, 43
Metropolitan West Side Elevated Railroad Company, 83
Michigan City, Ind., 17, 61, 79
Milwaukee, Wis., 83
Mohawk Valley Company, 29
Moore, F.T., 49, 53

Moore, George*, 23, *24*, 31, 37, 43, 45, 51, 55, 61, 73
Mott, Charles S., 9
Moulton, J.S., 81
Muncie, Ind., 83
Murdock, H.D., 55

- N -
Nester, J.A., 45
New Albany, Ind., *58*
New Haven, Conn., 81
Newport News and Hampton Railway Gas & Electric Co., 29
New Ross, Ind., 83
New York Central & Hudson River Railroad, 9, 19, 21, 27, 29, 35, 37, 71
New York City, 13, 29, 81, 83
New York, Ontario & Western Railroad, 9, 11, 26
New York State Railways, 9, 21, 29, 35, 37, 71, 85
Niagara Falls, NY., 15
Nicholl, H.A., 61
Nickel Plate Railroad, 38, 39, 69
Norfolk & Western Railway, 28
Northern Indiana Railway, 17
North Fairfield, Ohio, *94*
North, John, 71
Northwestern Elevated Railroad Company, 83
Norwalk, Ohio, *16*, 45, 47, 69, *90*

- O -
O'Hara, John*, 23, *24*, 31, *43*, 45, 51, 61, 73
Ohio Electric Railway, *6*, 45, 49, 50, 51, *52*, 53, *63*, 75, 87
Oneida Castle Station, *26*
Oneida, NY., 23, 33
Oneida Railway, 9, *10*, 19, 21, 23, *22, 24*, 25, *26*, 27, 28, 29, 31, 33, 45, 55, 67, 71, *72*, 73, 83, 87, 88 Car 502, 18, *21*, 23, 27, *30*, 31-73, *32, 33*, 38, *39*, 51, *52, 74*, 77, *80, 82*, 83, *84, 85*
Oneonta, NY., 13, 27, 81
Otsego & Herkimer Railroad, 27

- P -
Painesville, Ohio, 43
Palmer, R.W., 69
Parker, George W., 67
Payne, Fred E., 25, 27
Peck, Edward F., 29
Peck-Shannahan-Cherry, Inc., 29
Penn Central Railroad, 11
Pennsylvania & Ohio Railway, *40*, 41, 69
Peoria, Ill., 83
Peru, Ind., 13, 17, 37, 61, 79, 81, 83
Pittsburgh, Ohio, 79
Pittsfield, Mass., 81
Plymouth, Ohio, *14*, 47
Port Gibson, NY., *34*
Proctor, Thomas R., 11

- Q -
- R -
Radcliffe, George L., 43
Richmond, Ind., 53
Rochester & Syracuse Railroad, 25
Rochester, NY., 13, 19, 20, 21, 25, 27, 29, 31, 35, 37, 71, 67, 87 *Missing Track*, 19, 27, 35, 37, 71, *72*, 75, 81
Rochester, Syracuse & Eastern Railroad, 19, 29, *34*, 35, 37, *72*, 75, 81
Rockford & Interurban Railway, 83
Rockford, Ill., 83
Rome City Street Railway, 29

- S -
St. Louis, Mo., 81, 83
Sandusky, Norwalk & Mansfield Electric Railway, *14*, 16, 19, *46*, 47, 79, *94*
Sandusky, Ohio, *4*, 69, 81, 83
Savage Arms Company, 9, 31
Schachtel, William*, 25, 49, *50*
Scheider, E.F., 45

Schenectady, NY., 81
Schenectady Railway, 25
Schmock, E.L., 41, 43
Schultz, Paul Louis, 39
Seccaium Park, Ohio, *48*
Sellersburg, Ind., 55, 59
Sessions, Carrie R., 31, 51
Sessions, Fred W.*, 25, 31, 37, 51, 53
Seville, Ohio, 45, 79, 83
Seymour, Horatio, 9
Seymour, Ind., 55, 59, 79
Shelby, Ohio, 45, 47
Sherman, James Schoolcraft, 9
Snyder, Homer, 27
South Bend, Ind., 17, 79
Springfield, Ill., 83
Springfield, Mass., 81
Springfield, Ohio, 49, 83
Stanley, John J., 28, 29, 43, 69
Sweeney, Z.T., 55
Sweeting, Mrs. M.L., 37
Syracuse & Suburban Railroad, 29
Syracuse, Lake Shore & Northern, 35, 75
Syracuse Northern Electric Railway, 25
Syracuse, NY., 11, 19, 21, 23, 25, *26*, 28, 29, 33, 35, 45, 55, 71, *77, 80*, 81, *82*, 83, *84, 85*, 87
Syracuse Rapid Transit Ry., 21, 28, 29, 33
Syracuse Street Railroad Company, 28
Syracuse University, 28, 29, 35

- T -
Taft, William Howard, 9
Taylor, C.M., 61
Tedrahn, Fred, 83
Terre Haute, Ind., 79, 83
Terre Haute, Indianapolis & Eastern Traction Company, *53*
Tilton, B.E., 37
Toledo, Bowling Green & Southern Traction Company, 65
Toledo, Ohio, 20, 63, 65, 67, 69, 79, 83
Toledo Railways & Light Co., 65
Troy, NY., 81

- U -
Utica & Mohawk Valley Railway, 9, 21, 25, 27, 28, 29, 43, 73
Utica & Schenectady Railroad, 9
Utica Belt Line Street Railroad, 69
Utica Hotel, *see Hotel Utica*
Utica, NY., 9, *10*, 11, 19, 20, 21, 23, 25, 26, 27, 28, 29, 31, 33, 35, 41, 45, 55, 67, 69, 71, 73, 77, 81, 83, 85

- V -
Van Valkenburgh, E.C., 81
Van Zandt, A.D.B., 67
Vickery, Ohio, 69

- W -
Wabash, Ind., 61, 81
Wardman, Palmer, 41, 69
Warsaw, Ind., 81
Weedsport, NY., 35
West Shore Railroad, 11, 21, 23, 27, 29, 31, 33, 71
Western Ohio Railway, 63, *64*, 65
Whiffen, B. Allen*, 25
Whysall, George, 47
Wicks, Charles W.*, 31, 71
Williams, Charles L.*, 25, *50*
Willoughby, Ohio, *42*, 43, 45, *68*
Wilson, B.E., 37, 71
Winona Interurban Ry., 13, *17*, 37, 61, 81
Wright, Edward J., 25, 27, 31, 35, 67

- X -
- Y -
Youngstown, Ohio, 79

- Z -
Zanesville, Ohio, 15, 79

* Also see photo on page 32.